In Van Gogh's Own Words

THE CONNECTION BETWEEN THE WORD AND THE IMAGE

ANNE DUPRÉ

To Daniel, Roger, and Mary

Aurora Books, an imprint of Eco-Justice Press, L.L.C.

Aurora Books
www.ecojusticepress.com

In Van Gogh's Own Words
The connection between the word and the image
by Anne Dupré

Library of Congress Control Number: 2021949486
ISBN 978-1-945432-71-2

On the cover

Self-Portrait (1889), one of Van Gogh's greatest, was painted during his stay at the asylum in Saint-Rémy-de-Provence only months before his death. Clearly not merely a depiction of his physical self, this deeply introspective work is a distinct psychological study created during a brief respite from the mental breakdown he had been experiencing.

I'm trying to do as well as certain painters whom I've greatly admired... What I'm seeking in it is not resemblance, but rather the expression of emotions that grip me when I look in the mirror" (September 1889).

The turbulent, swirling brushstrokes of the background and coat create a visual expression of tension. Looking out at the viewer, the steady gaze of his piercing blue eyes conveys the storm within and serves as a powerful glimpse into his soul.

His masterful use of color enhances this inner turmoil. The greenish hue of his skin gives him a sickly, melancholic appearance, and the red-orange beard and hair suggest the fiery temperament of a soul in distress. Depending on the light, the shimmering blue-green background shifts to a subtle blue tone—a color he associated with infinity and spirituality.

The blue sky is all I see beyond the iron bars... it's like infinity, a kind of peace (April, 1888).

In the shadow of death, "the sky, infinity, a kind of peace" had to be a dominant thought. For a brief moment, this profoundly personal portrait rescued a tormented genius in deep pain.

The art historian Meyer Shapiro wrote, "What is most important is that Van Gogh converted all this aspiration and anguish into his art, which thus became the first example of truly personal art, art as a deeply lived means of spiritual deliverance or transformation.

Illustrations

Irises

Irises and Butterfly – Hiroshige

Langlois Bridge at Arles with Women

The Drum Bridge at Meguro and Sunset- Hokusai

A View of Arles

The Courtyard of the Hospital at Arles

Pollard Willows at Sunset

Olive Trees with Cut Trunk

The Pine Grove of Miho in Suruga Province -Hiroshige

Olive Trees with Yellow Sky and Sun

Women Picking Olives

A View from a Pork Shop in Arles

At Eternity's Gate

Self-Portrait as a Bonze

Portrait of Hokusai - Keisai Eisen

Portrait with a Bandaged Ear

The Peasant (Patience Escalier

The Poet (Portrait of Eugene Boch

The Portrait of Dr. Gachet

The Night Café

Terrace at Night

The Yellow House

In the Bedroom

The Old Tower and Cemetery

The Church at Auvers

Wheatfield with Crows

Tree Roots in Sandy Ground

Tree Roots

Table of Contents

The imaged word, it is, that holds
Hushed willows anchored in its glow.

Hart Crane

Introduction

For he grew up before him like a young plant
And like a root out of dry ground;
He had no form of comeliness that we should look at him
And no beauty that we should desire him
He was despised and abandoned by men,
A man of great pain and familiar with sickness;
And like one from whom people hide their faces,
He was despised, and we had no regard for Him.
However, it was our sicknesses that He Himself bore,
And our pains that He carried;

Isaiah 53:2-4

Inside me there is still a calm, pure harmony and music.

Despite his struggles with mental illness, loneliness, rejection, and poverty, Vincent Van Gogh's artistic endeavors gave his life profound meaning. His letters primarily to his brother Theo—a treasure of revelation—tell us so much about his art and his personal challenges.

Even though I am often in a mess, inside me there is still a calm, pure harmony and music. (July 1882).

His connection to the world around him—ether in the Netherlands, Paris, Arles, or Auvers—is always deeply personal. The beauty he saw in nature and humanity brought an artistic clarity to his paintings that viewers all over the world have found so deeply engaging and profoundly moving.

Raised in a devout Protestant household, his father and grandfather both pastors, Van Gogh at the age of 24 enrolled at the University of Amsterdam to prepare for his role as a Protestant minister. After failing the entrance exam, he entered the Missionary Training School in Brussels. His work as a missionary with the impoverished coal miners in the Borinage led to his disillusionment and rejection of traditional religious dogma. Experiencing a godliness in the dignity of the working people, he shifted from conventional religious beliefs to a broader, more personal, and mystical understanding of spirituality

His turning away from the traditional religious dogma followed by his father, a pastor in the Dutch Reformed Church. is reflected in *Still Life with Bible* (1885).

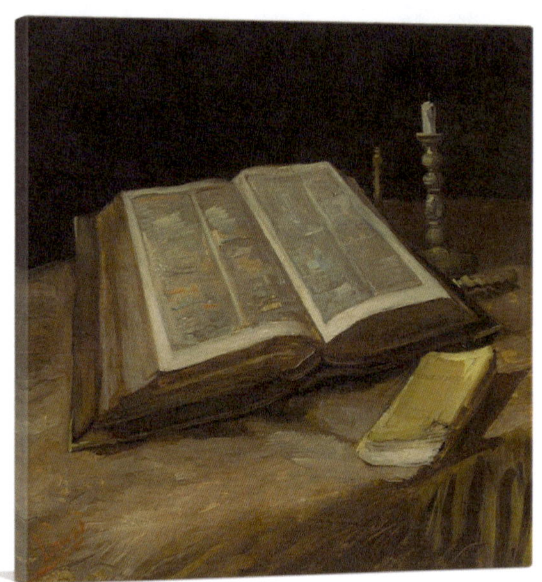

Created shortly after his father's death, the painting features his father's Bible believed to be opened to Isaiah 53:2-4, the "Suffering Servant Song," often interpreted as a reference to Van Gogh (see the passage in the introduction). One cannot deny that his life, both emotionally and spiritually, was one of rejection and suffering, and he was always deeply inspired by the idea of bearing his suffering as a way to serve others.

Next to the Bible, the copy of Zola's *The Joy of Living*, a more modern view of life, clearly reflects Van Gogh's struggle between the faith of his upbringing and the intellectual ideas he was now embracing. His father, a man of deep, traditional beliefs, vehemently disapproved of Vincent's life during this period.

Father does not understand me and thinks I am a madman or a religious fanatic or a man of bad character (July 1880).

The extinguished candle standing next to the Bible can be seen both as a symbol of the end of his father's life and the end of Van Gogh's complex relationship with his father and the faith of his youth. In the last years of his life, his unconventional religious beliefs now replacing traditional dogma, Van Gogh came to see the sky as "something up there" that couldn't be named. Yet he continued to experience a profound sense of spiritual wonder—a faith entirely his own.

For my part I know nothing with any certainty, but the sight of the stars makes me dream (July 1888).

Although he was not directly trained in Eastern philosophy and never mentioned having read Basho, the 17th century haiku poet and painter, his admiration for Japanese art (including a huge collection of ukiyo-e- woodblock prints) suggests that he possessed a deep understanding—whether intuitively or consciously—of Eastern Zen thought.

> *Learn about a pine tree from a pine tree,*
>
> *And about a bamboo stalk from a bamboo stalk.*
>
> *Basho*

Basho believed one must detach the mind from self and enter into the object, sharing its delicate life and its feelings, allowing himself to become one with the subject in order to authentically capture its essence—a powerful expression that true artistic understanding comes from direct observation of and intimate relationship with nature. He held that all who achieved artistic greatness possess one essential quality: "a mind to obey nature, to be one with nature, throughout the four seasons of the year."

Van Gogh always sought to engage with nature directly. He closely observed the uniqueness of each sunflower, wheatfield, iris, cypress, and olive grove through the four seasons—in the brilliant light of the radiant sun and beneath a starry sky.

I see that nature has told me something, has spoken to me . . . and that I have put it down in shorthand. In my shorthand there may be words that cannot be deciphered, there may be mistakes or gaps; but there is something of what wood or beach or figure has told me in it, and it is not the tame or conventional language derived from a studied manner or a system rather than from nature itself (October 1885).

His process of painting quickly was a way of instinctively recording the essence of what nature revealed to him, a kind of "shorthand" charged with emotional and spiritual resonance. It wasn't about reproducing what the eye could see, but about making visible what lies beneath—the unseen spirit animating all things.

What cannot be seen with the eye

But that whereby the eye can see:

Know that alone . . .be the eternal spirit.

The Upanishads

I let myself be saturated with the air of the little mountains and the orchards; this much gained, I shall wait and see. My ambition is truly limited to a few clods of earth, some sprouting wheat, an olive grove, a cypress... (July 1888).

This connection to the natural world underscores the profound influence nature had on him—a sensibility that aligns closely with Zen principles.

A meadow full of very yellow buttercups, a ditch with iris plants with green leaves, with purple flowers, the town in the background, some grey willow trees—a strip of blue sky. . . That would really be a Japanese dream, you know (May,1888).

He often stated how he was not "seeking for fame and success," but simply immersing himself in the beauty of the moment. Nature and humanity spoke to Van Gogh in their own language, reinforcing his spiritual connection to the world around him. The divine could be experienced in the beauty of the natural world, in the dignity of the working people, and in the act of creating art that conveyed this truth. At the age of 27 he dedicated himself wholly to the lifelong pursuit of revealing these truths through his paintings.

I felt my energy revive, and said to myself, in spite of everything I shall rise again: I will take up my pencil, which I have forsaken in my great discouragement, and I will go on with my drawing. From that moment everything has seemed transformed for me (September 1880).

His life's mission became a search for how to integrate his renewed religious awareness, love of nature, the world of literature and ideas, and concern for humanity into his art. As Meyer Shapiro wrote, "Art was a choice made for personal salvation after he had failed in another hope, a religious mission as an evangelist among the poor miners of the Borinage."

In Van Gogh's Own Words

There is something noble in labor.

One of Van Gogh's earliest paintings, *The Potato Eaters* (1885), focuses on the dignity of the working people.

I feel that there is a something deeper, something more sublime, in all of this work that speaks of life and human dignity... I want to create art that expresses the dignity of the working class. I want to show how beautiful and sacred everything is, even in its most humble and neglected forms (August 1882).

In a room dimly lit by a single oil lamp, a peasant family sits around a table eating potatoes, a simple act, essential to their survival and deeply revealing of their poverty. Like Jean-Francois Millet (1814–1875), a leading figure of the Barbizon School whom he greatly admired, Van Gogh sought to depict peasant life with empathy, dignity, and quiet gravity. This admiration, reflected in the earthy palette of brown, greens, and grays, and in Van Gogh's signature style of thick rough brush strokes clearly creates a somber atmosphere offering an intimate look into the wear and hardships of peasant life. Enhanced by the harsh light cast by the oil lamp, their haggard faces emphasize the struggles of everyday living, and their rough gnarled hands provide a powerful symbol of their manual labor and their connection to the soil.

I wanted to make it so that one would get the idea that these people eating their potatoes by the light of their little lamp have tilled the earth themselves with these hands they are putting in the dish, and so it speaks of manual labor and—that they have thus honestly earned their food (April 1885).

In this simple act of eating, Van Gogh conveys his deep respect for the working class.

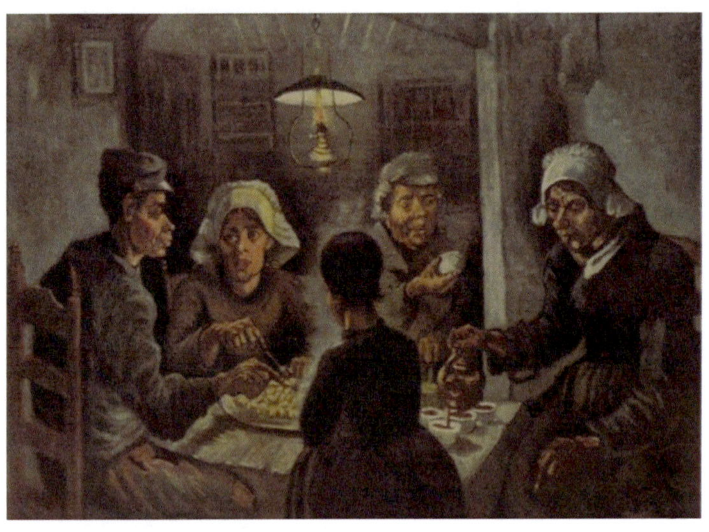

I always think that the best way to know God is to love many things. I always think that when we see the image of unutterable desolation, of loneliness, of poverty and misery, the end or extreme of all things, then it is that the thought of God comes to us (July 1880)

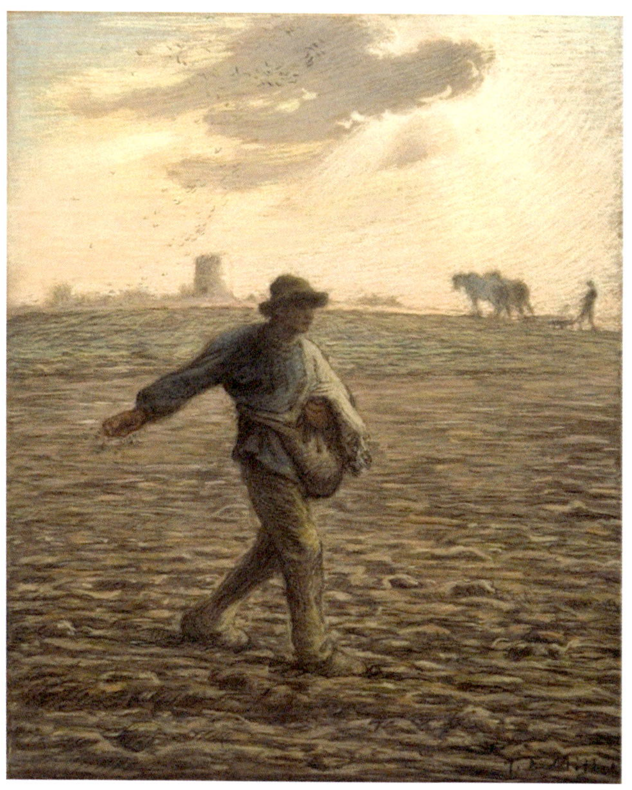

In his effort to create art that expressed the divinity in the land and in the laborers who till the soil, he painted several Sowers. Inspired by Jean-Francois Millet's *The Sower,* Vincent transformed *The Sower at Sunset* (1888) into his own unique, spiritual vision.

A Sower -- I see him from my window – he stands against the blazing disc of the sun. And in it, I see the meaning of work and life, the endless cycle (June,1888).

Set against a radiant sun that dominates the sky, the lone farmer sows his seeds in a vast field vibrant in colors of bright yellows, deep purples, and rich blues. By this time, he had lived in Paris and had been introduced to the impressionist's world of light and color.

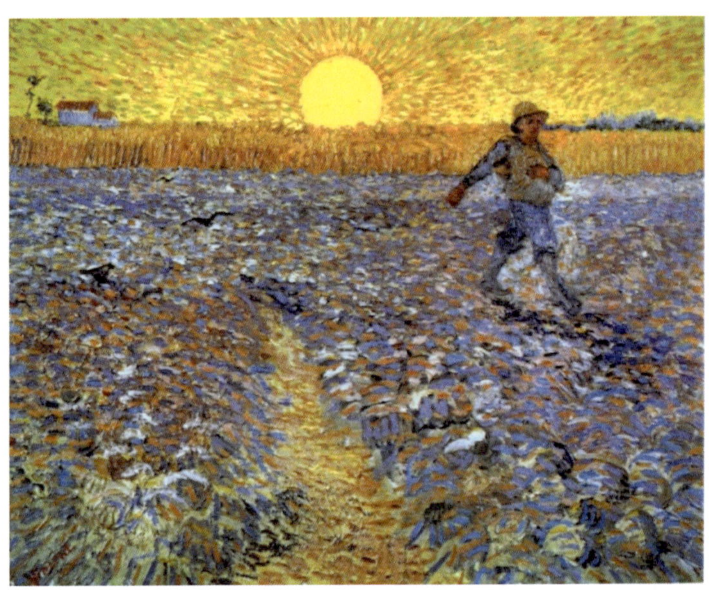

I am always in hope of making a discovery there, to express the love of two lovers by a marriage of two complementary colors, their mingling and their opposition, the mysterious vibrations of kindred tones. To express hope by some star, the eagerness of a soul by a sunset radiance (June 1888).

For Van Gogh, color was a powerfully expressive and spiritual tool. Bold and unrestrained, his use of color has inspired generations of artists. As John Elderfield notes in *The Wild Beast,* his use of "pure color" had a profound impact on Henri Matisse, Andre Derain, and Maurice de Vlaminck, the early 20th century founders of Fauvism. This influence extends far beyond Fauvism. Modern artists, such as Picasso, Hockney, Miro—and the list goes on—have absorbed and reinterpreted Van Gogh's emotive palette in their own unique voices.

It is colour not locally true from the point of view of the trompe d'oeil realist, but colour to suggest some emotion of an ardent temperament. (September 1888).

This emotional intensity is vividly evident in the glowing sun, a symbol of life-giving energy, shining down on the sower, suggesting a spiritual presence and the promise of future harvests.

For I see in this (sower)—*a vague figure fighting like a devil in the midst of the heat to get to the end of his task—I see in him the image of death. . . But there is nothing sad in this death, it goes its way in broad daylight with a sun flooding everything with a light of pure gold* (July 1889).

There is nothing mournful in this passing. Life, labor, and death, the inevitable journey intertwine, and the sower is just one small link in the greater chain of being, while "death is the entrance into to another light, one that is eternal."

With a profound sensitivity to the human condition, and now shaped by a renewed spiritual vision, Van Gogh poured into *The Sower (with a Tree)* (1888) a message that he deeply felt.

There is something noble in labor, something that touches upon the divine. One feels closer to God when engaged in honest work, when the hands are busy shaping something real. It is through purpose, just as a painter finds his in the strokes of his brush. To work is to pray (September 1880).

From his early awakening working with the miners in the Borinage, Van Gogh strove to express the godliness in the dignity of the working people.

I'd like to paint men or women with that je ne sais quoi of the eternal, of which the halo used to be the symbol (August 1888).

The golden sun haloing the dark silhouette of the sower touches upon this divinity, and the unnatural hues in the intense striated greenish-yellow sky over a deep purple field surround the saintly laborer in a mystical atmosphere.

To the right of the sower, a truncated tree reflects the potential for growth in this endless cycle of sowing and harvesting. Though cut off, the tree stands prominently in the foreground still flowering, suggesting perseverance and resilience. Like the tree, the lone figure's saintly labor will be rewarded with growth. The rich color palette expresses this joy of renewal in the noble act of scattering seeds, the "je ne sais quoi of the eternal."

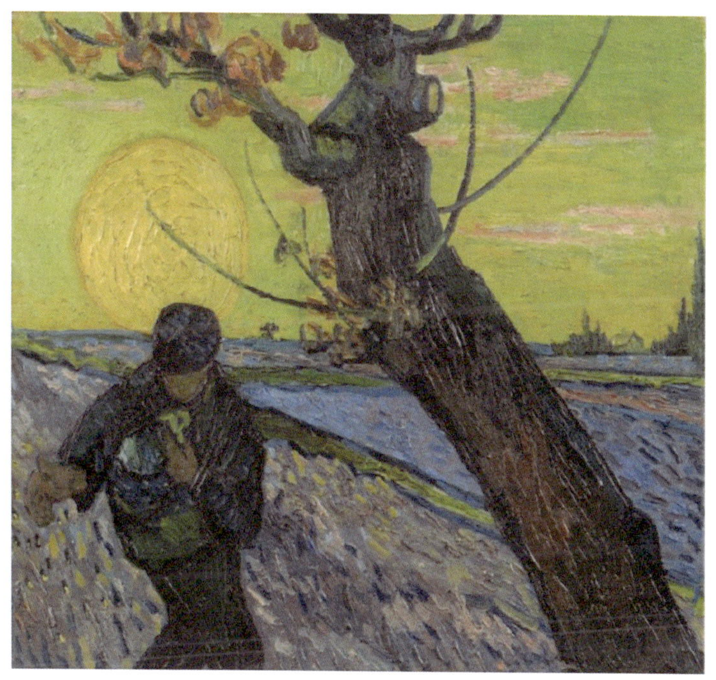

The Siesta (1890), painted while he was at Saint Paul de Mausole, the asylum at Saint Remy de Provence, is based on *a La Méridienne* by Jean Francois Millet.

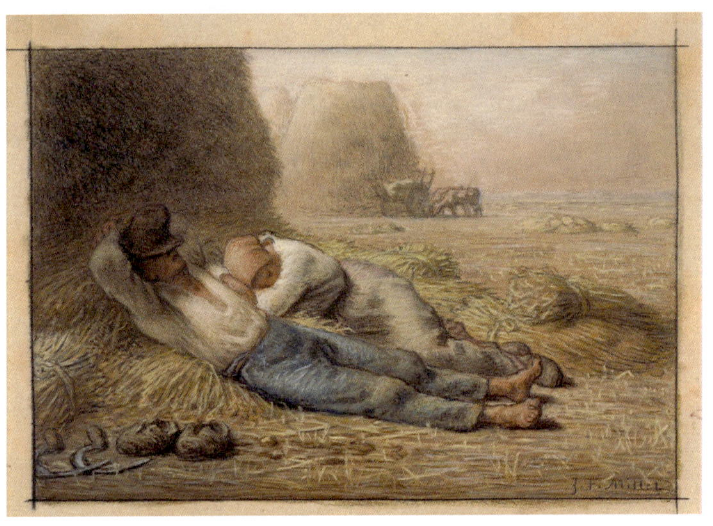

I've also done after Millet a La Méridienne. The violet shadows of a sunlit wall on the ground of sand with the white clothing of the sleeping peasant couple make a whole that's quite colorful (January, 1889)

Always attuned to the expressive power of color, Van Gogh's masterful use of a vibrant palette—warm yellow wheat, rich blue sky, and earth tones—shapes a unique vision that beautifully captures the couple's peaceful moment of respite.

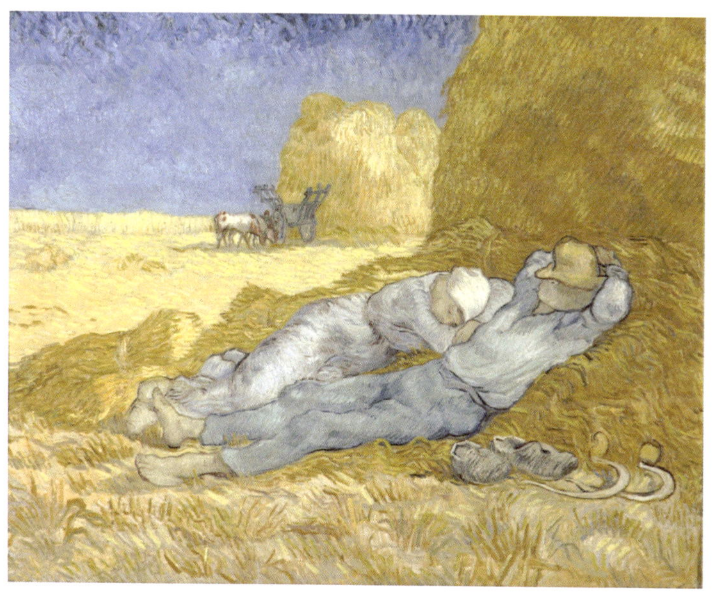

In a letter to his sister Wilhemina he wrote,

In nature something similar in what happens in Wagner's music, which, though played by a big orchestra, is nonetheless intimate. Only when making a choice one prefers sunny and colourful effects, and there is nothing that prevents me from thinking that in the future many painters will go and work in tropical countries. You will be able to get an idea of the revolution of painting when you think, for instance, of the brightly coloured Japanese pictures that one sees everywhere, landscapes and figure (March 1888).

Choosing to use swirling, short brushstrokes brings the entire field to life, and the muted tones of the couples clothing unite with the soft blue sky and yellow wheat, a reflection that the farmers are one with the land.

Two scythes, a cart, and a pair of worn muddy shoes beside the reclining couple suggest the farmers have been working hard harvesting and are well deserving of this rest. Their world dominated by toil becomes a meditation on the rhythm of the human experience—work and rest—that brings satisfaction and spiritual fulfillment—"To work is to pray."

Although exhausted, they look relaxed and at peace, the peace that comes with a job well done. This awareness brings dignity and even divinity to the laborers and their labor—"There is something noble in labor, something that touches upon the divine"—and momentary calmness to Van Gogh's troubled mind.

I mean painting and, to my mind, particularly painting peasant life, gives peace of mind, even though one has a lot of scraping along and wretchedness on the outside of life (June 1885).

Van Gogh's communion with nature was always deeply personal. The godliness that he found in the dignity of work could be experienced everywhere in the beauty of the natural world.

This morning I saw the country from my window a long time before sunrise, with nothing but the morning star, which looked very big. . .all that it has of intimacy, all that vast peace and majesty . . . (September 1888).

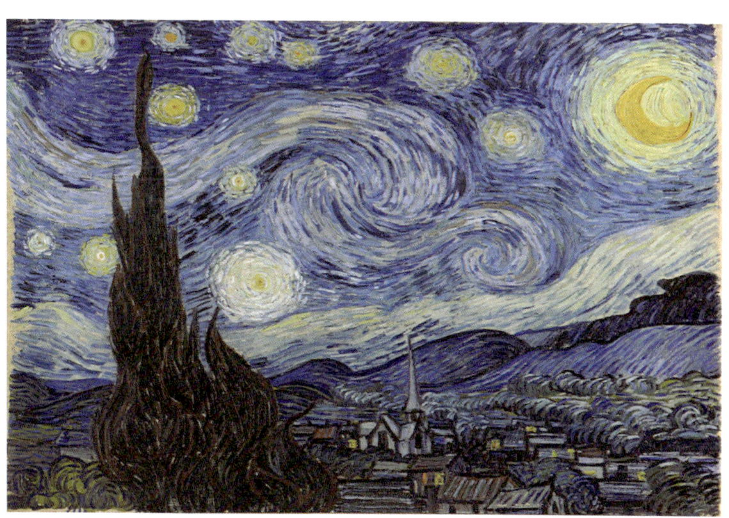

This moment before dawn captures the wonder that permeates one of Vincent's most famous paintings. Rooted in his imagination as a homage to nature, *Starry Night* (1889) transcends traditional religion.

It does me good to do difficult things. That doesn't stop me having a terrible need for—shall I say the word—religion. Then I go outside at night to paint the stars (September 1888).

Painted in the Asylum at St. Remy when he was struggling with depression, the moon, the stars, and the cypress become a symbol of his spiritual salvation.   Emphasizing only the essential in this dynamic night scene, the quiet village—barely noticeable—lies below a vibrant swirling blue sky with glittering yellow stars and a golden moon.

And I even do my best not to give details—for then the dreaminess goes out of it. . . art is something which, although produced by human hands, is not created by these hands . . . but something which wells up from a deeper source in our souls (March 1884).

Behold, I have dreamed a dream more

And, behold the sun and the moon and

The eleven stars made obeisance to me.

(Genesis 37:9)

Rejecting art based on human technique, color and movement dominate this image. The interaction of deep blues, bright yellows, and gold creates a cosmic energy, an invitation to contemplate the divine and the infinite.

I'm trying to express the great infinite. The whole universe seems to me to be within the bounds of what I can paint (September 1888).

Presiding over the village church in the distance, a large flame-like cypress, often interpreted as a symbol of death and eternity, reaches for the sky. Following the cypress like a bridge between the earth and the sky and traveling with the stars swirling over rolling hills and the moon pulsating in an orb of golden light becomes a journey through the end of the cycle of life to a new light, the "eternal."

Someday death will take us to another star . . . One that we can see twinkling in the sky. This life is only a kind of light and death is the entrance into another light, one that is eternal (October, 1879.

These words reveal the deep spiritual undercurrent that runs through Van Gogh's art. Recognizing this, the French Symbolist critic Gabriel-Albert Aurier, in his 1890 article *The Isolated Ones: Vincent Van Gogh*, portrayed him as a visionary and symbolist painter. Emphasizing the expressive and spiritual qualities of his work, he wrote:

"Beneath skies that sometimes dazzle like faceted sapphires or turquoises. . . The streaming of every conceivable effect of light, in heavy, flaming, burning atmospheres that seem to be exhaled from fantastic furnaces where gold and diamonds and similar gems are volatilized—there is the disquieting and disturbing display of strange nature, that is at once entirely realistic, and yet almost supernatural. . .

In almost all his canvases, Aurier wrote, "beneath this morphic exterior . . . beneath this matter that is very much matter, there lies, for the spirit that knows how to find it, a thought, an idea, and this Idea, the essential substratum of the work, is, at the same time, its efficient and final cause."

This deep, underlying idea—what Aurier called the "efficient and final cause"—also shaped Van Gogh's fascination with Japanese art, which he viewed not simply as a stylistic influence but as a spiritual and emotional ideal.

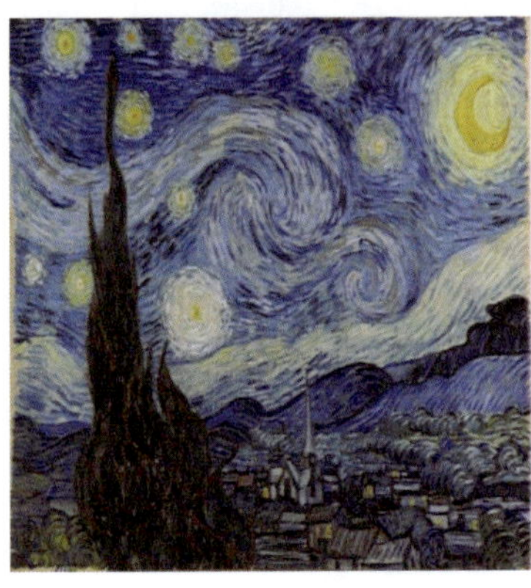 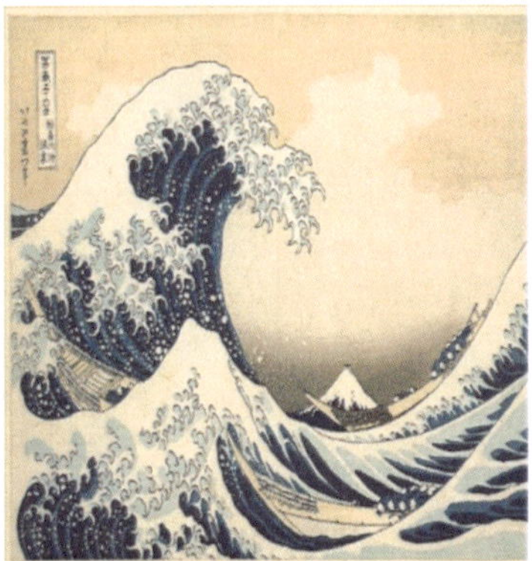

Separated by time and culture, *The Great Wave off Kanagawa* and *The Starry Night*—emblems of world art—transform universal human emotions into something beautiful and enduring. While Hokusai's *Great Wave* captures the overwhelming power of nature, Van Gogh's swirling sky, alive with motion and feeling, reflects his inner world. Both become mirrors of the soul, revealing the depths of human experience,

In *Starry Night over the Rhone* (1888), Van Gogh elevates nature beyond its physical reality, taking a simple night scene into the cosmic and spiritual realm.

Under the great starlit vault of heaven, there's a feeling that life is indeed something earnest and grand. One can't help feeling that there's something higher than ourselves, the mystery of eternity is placed above the world (September 1888).

With the stars radiating halos of yellow and white and the shimmering gaslights from the houses along the shore beaming across the dark velvety blue water, the mesmerizing scene pulsates with cosmic energy. In the foreground a couple share a quiet moment under the vast cosmic beauty, and the grandeur of the night becomes a poignant meditation on the union of human life with the universe.

Anne Dupré

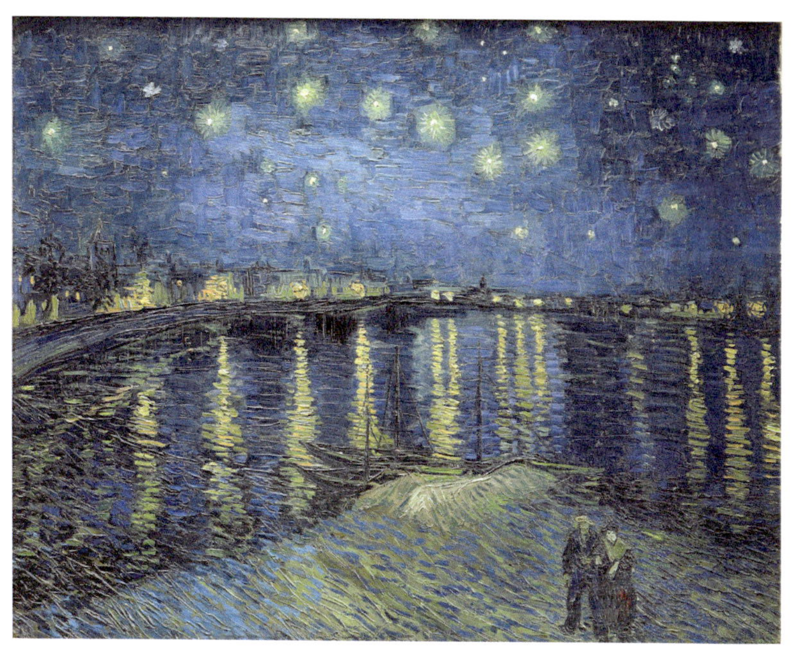

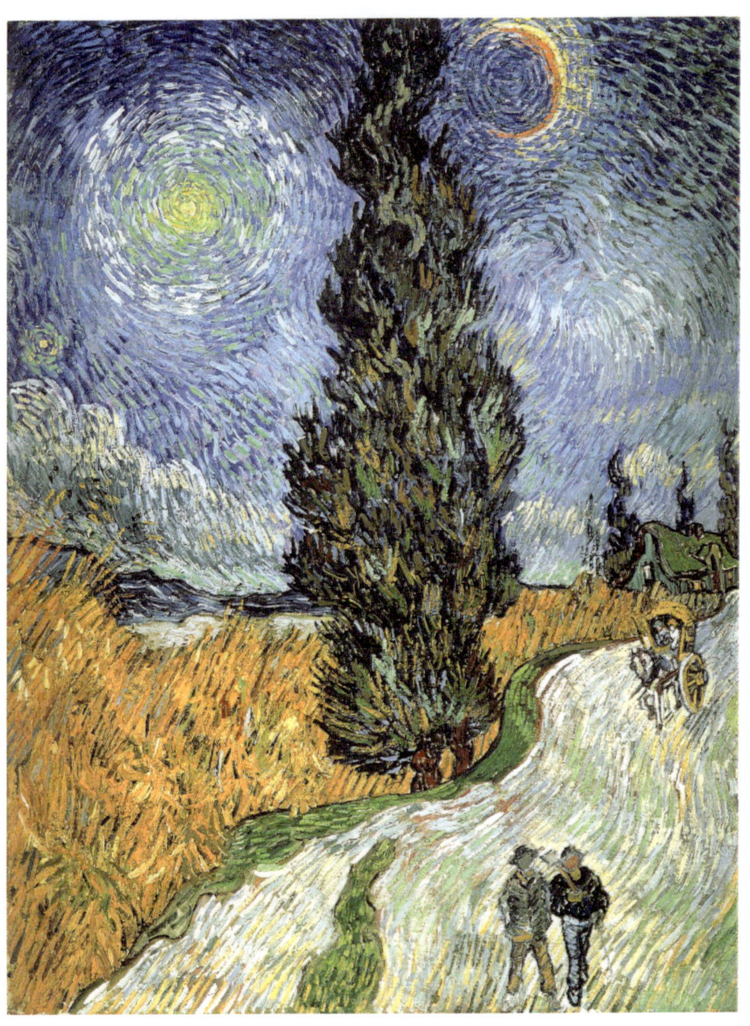

Always a source of inspiration, the sky remained one of Van Gogh's most powerful motifs, along with his fascination with cypress trees.

But the cypresses still preoccupy me, I'd like to do something with them like the canvases of the sunflowers, because it astonishes me that no one has yet done them as I see them. It's beautiful as regards lines and proportions, like an Egyptian obelisk. And the green is of such a distinguished quality. It's the dark patch in a sun-drenched landscape, but it's one of the most interesting dark notes, the most difficult to get exactly right that I can imagine (July, 1889).

In *Road with Cypresses* (1890), the dominant cypress, a symbol of eternity and death, stands tall in the center of a scene alive with movement, that "dark patch . . . but it's one of the most interesting dark notes." Illuminated by a crescent moon to the right and a large radiant star on the left, the towering cypress, reaches up into the "eternal" space.

The two figures in the foreground and a cart in the background continue down a steep winding road. The unpredictable turns foreshadow the problems they will encounter. Beneath this swirling canopy of the infinite, their travels take on the significance of a life's journey. The soaring cypress, the golden star in a circle of white, and a red-orange crescent moon radiating with cosmic energy promise them hope, a hope that Vincent held onto through most of his life.

The energetic brushstrokes and vibrant color palette of yellows and red-oranges contrasting with rich blues and greens create a night scene of intense emotion that expresses the significance of their journey. This masterful use of brushstrokes and color reveals the inner workings of Van Gogh's mind.

I seek to express not only what is before my eyes but what is within me—my emotions, my experience of the world (August 1888).

Deeply troubled at this time, he stands before the canvas and paints an existential view of life's journey, a night journey guided only by the crescent moon and a star whose light offers hope along the chosen path.

The great thing is to gather the light from the flame and then pass it on; for we do not really die but go from one light into another (October 1879).

Meyer Shapiro wrote, for Van Gogh, "the artist is no longer a neutral observer, but someone who transforms what he sees into a deeply personal vision."

In *La Berceuse (1890)*, one of five versions of Van Gogh's portraits of Madame Roulin, the dichotomy of darkness and light delves deeply, expressing both a consoling image of motherhood and the existential reality of life.

In a letter to his brother Theo, Vincent discussed his inspiration.

When I heard about "the Icelandic fishermen, men exposed to all dangers, alone on the sad sea, I envisioned painting a picture that sailors, who are at once children and martyrs, seeing it in the cabin of their boat should feel the old sense of cradling come over them and remember their own lullabies (January 1880).

Set against a green background filled with colorful flowers, Madame Roulin evokes life and renewal. Her rich deep green dress contrasts with the warm tones of the floral background

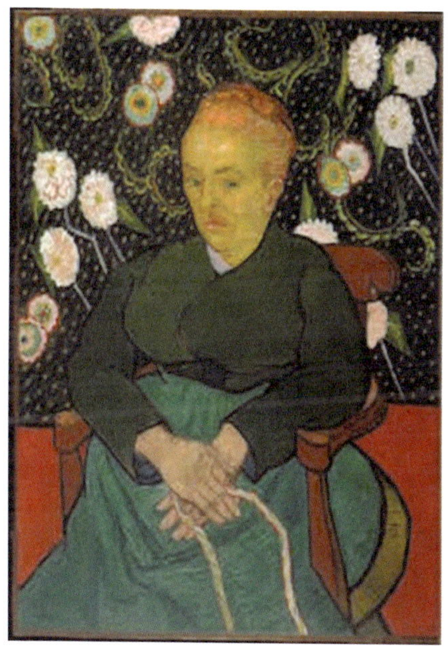

and her red-orange hair. The vibrant color palette enhances the emotional and expressive power of the portrait. Van Gogh hoped people could hear a melody in the vivid and harmonious use of color. He planned to surround this tender rhythmic vision with flowers.

You know that the peony is Jeannin's, and the hollyhock belongs to Quost (contemporary artists), but the sunflower is mine ... The whole thing will be a symphony ... I'm working at it every morning from sunrise. If it succeeds it will be like a piece of stained- glass in a Gothic Church (August, 1888).

While firmly rooted in his post-impressionist style, the bold outline, decorative background, and sunflowers on each side" echo medieval influence—like a "piece of stained glass." Although always deeply inspired by Japanese artists' use of bold outlines and flat areas of color, he was also drawn to the way medieval artists chose expressive forms over strict naturalism—favoring symbolism rather than realism

Madame Roulin will be surrounded by sunflowers. A strong composition, with large areas of soft color. I want to paint this triptych with great care because I see it as a new departure in my work. In this, I wish to combine my interest in the human figure with an

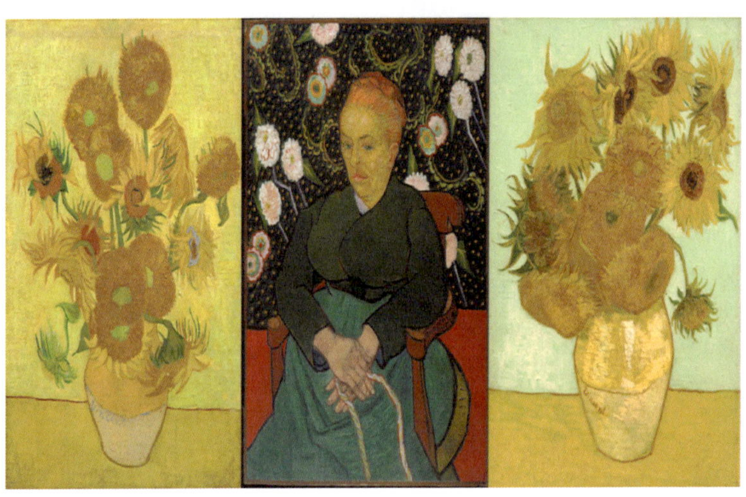

appreciation for the natural world, and to convey my own emotional state in relation to these subjects (March 1889).

He had "great faith in its power to speak to people" Beneath the beauty and light, the sunflowers, yellow and ocher, symbolizing joy, warmth, and vitality, are in various stages of the cycle of life—full bloom, fading, and dying. In placing Madame Roulin between the sunflowers, Van Gogh expresses a deep awareness of the human condition, reinforcing the cyclical nature of existence. The Japanese aesthetic mono no aware—an awareness of the fleeting nature of life, a gentle sadness at its passing, but a deeper appreciation born from this transience—resonates quietly throughout this work.

I hope that you will see that it is not merely a subject of motherhood, but a more profound exploration of rest, tenderness, and peace . . . I have great faith in its power to speak to people, especially to women, who will understand the emotional and symbolic significance of the piece (September 1889).

Underlying its vibrant surface lies a profound truth. Like Atropos, one of the three Greek goddesses of fate who cuts the thread of life, Madame Roulin scissoring her fingers around the cradle rope, her gaze intensely absorbed in thought, almost burdened with the knowledge of life's transience, is fully aware of the infant's destiny.

I'd rather paint people's eyes than cathedrals, for there is something in the eyes that isn't in the cathedral... the soul of a person (September, 1888).

Her intense gaze has become the portal into the symbolic heart of the painting—an in-depth understanding of the human condition.

There is sorrow in the hour when a man is born into the world, and there is sorrow in the hour when he dies, but there is also a great joy in both. (July, 1880).

The power and resonance Van Gogh found in the books he read shaped his vision and moved his brush across the canvas.

I have a passionate desire to grasp the things that exist in books, in people, in the countryside. That is why I feel drawn to the painters who express something more than just an arrangement of colors— who express a feeling, just as a writer expresses a thought in words (October, 1879).

On February 18, 1890 he wrote to his brother about his fascination with Walt Whitman's poetry.

And while reading Whitman, I say to myself: how much that

man has seen! And how he has felt (February 1890).

These lines from Whitman's "Out of the Cradle Endlessly Rocking" are so relevant to a deeper understanding of *La Berceuse.*

> ***Out of the mocking-birds throat,***
>
> ***. . . . .***
>
> ***The message there arous'd***
>
> ***. . . . . the destiny of me.***
>
> ***. . . . .***
>
> ***Creeping thence steadily up to my ears and laving me softly all over,***
>
> ***Death, death, death, death, death.***
>
> ***(Or like some old crone rocking the cradle, swathed in sweet garments, bendng aside,)***
>
> ***The sea whisper'd me.***

While Whitman grappled with the theme of death, he saw life as an endless cycle of death and renewal, where the self is never truly lost but transformed.

> ***I bequeath myself to the dirt to grow from the grass I love, If you want me again look for me under your boot-soles. (from Song of Myself)***

For Vincent death was not an ending. Like Christian's perilous journey that ultimately brought him to the celestial city in *The Pilgrim's Progress*, a book he read many times and referenced in his first sermon in 1876, he had a firm belief that his life's journey, painful as it was, would end in celestial joy. He referred often to his life as "sorrowful, yet always rejoicing" Corinthians 6:10.

Our life is a pilgrim's progress. We are strangers on the earth, but we walk with hope toward a better land. Every struggle, every sorrow, brings us a step closer to the light. . . One must not delude oneself—we are pilgrims and strangers on the earth. . . There is a time to search and a time to lose, a time to keep and a time to cast away. But we, who believe in God, walk as strangers and pilgrims toward a better homeland. (November 1877).

Although his relationship with his faith became increasingly personal—a more mystical understanding of spirituality—in a letter to his brother in 1888 he reflects again on spiritual perseverance echoing the Bible.

I tell myself that in the long run we're not walking toward ruin but toward a better future. If we don't believe in that, we're lost (December 1888).

These words, a reflection on hope and perseverance in the face of uncertainty, resonate with Hebrews 11:13–16.

> *. . . . they were strangers and pilgrims on the earth. For they that say such things declare plainly that they seek a country.*
>
> *. . . . . .*
> *But now they desire a better country, that is, an heavenly: Wherefore God is not ashamed to be called their God:*
>
> *for he hath prepared for them a city.*
> *—Hebrews 11:13–16*

For Van Gogh, the figure of the pilgrim became a powerful metaphor—the artist as a spiritual seeker, wandering through darkness toward something luminous and eternal.

That same spirit of hopeful endurance—and a deep understanding that love and loss are forever intwined—is vividly present in *La Berceuse*, where the tenderness of the mother figure, the rhythmic floral background, the vibrant color palette, and quiet serenity suggest not only comfort and warmth, but a trust in something greater—something "eternal."

In this inevitable face of death, Madam Roulin, a modern-day Madonna serving as a meditation on the fragility of existence, has the power to bring comfort to the Icelandic fishermen and consolation to all who understand her emotional and symbolic significance.

In the late 19th century, the impact of Japanese art, culture, and aesthetics grew among Western European artists. Seeking an alternative to the Renaissance tradition, the unusual viewpoints and flattened space of this art inspired European painters to experiment with composition and new ideas of perspective. Embracing this new movement, Van Gogh began collecting ukiyo-e woodblock prints and found inspiration in their principle of harmony in nature, often depicted in a symbolic and poetic way. He came to believe that by focusing on small things, you would open up not only to the vastness of nature but to a deeper understanding of life.

And then, having drawn that blade of grass, one should not be discouraged, but proceed to draw every blade of grass in that meadow, studying each one carefully . . . Look a blade of grass, how well that is drawn, how free and easy in its movements, how well it expresses both shape and the life of the thing (September 1888).

The woodblock prints closely influenced not only his subject matter but also the way he approached composition, color, line, and perspective. This aesthetic influenced his art until the end of his life.

When Vincent moved to Arles in 1888, he wrote to Theo that he hoped to create a "Japan of the South."

We like Japanese paintings, we've felt its influence—all the Impressionists have that in common—therefore we aren't far from believing that we can easily go there in our minds. My dear brother, you know, I sometimes regret that I can't just go right there, but alas, it is quite difficult. So I say to myself, let's look for a bit of Japan here in the South! . . . You know that I have a boundless admiration for Japanese art. It is something quite different from what we are used to, and it makes us return to nature, despite its simplifications. I have just done a study after a Japanese print—Hiroshige's 'Bridge in the Rain.' The color combinations are vivid, and I have tried to enhance them, to make them speak even more forcefully. There is something in these prints that makes me feel calm, as if I am stepping into a different world—one that is simpler and more harmonious than our own . . . The Japanese instinctively know how to compose with color and line. I am beginning to understand that by studying them, we can learn to see nature differently. . . "I hope you will like this one. It is not a mere copy, but rather an interpretation, my own way of seeing through their eyes (September 1888).

Influenced by the impressionists and his "boundless admiration for Japanese art," color played a vital role in all of Van Gogh's paintings. He moved from the Netherlands to the South of France hoping to capture the brighter light and vibrant colors. While living in Arles, he described how colors could be arranged like musical notes.

Color is the keyboard, the eyes are the harmonies, the soul is the piano with many strings. The artist is the hand that plays, touching one key or another, to cause vibrations in the soul" (July 1888).

In choosing to recreate *A Portrait of a Bridge (after Hiroshige) (1887)* in the denser medium of oil and make the color combination more intense, Van Gogh shows his deep understanding of the expressive power of color.

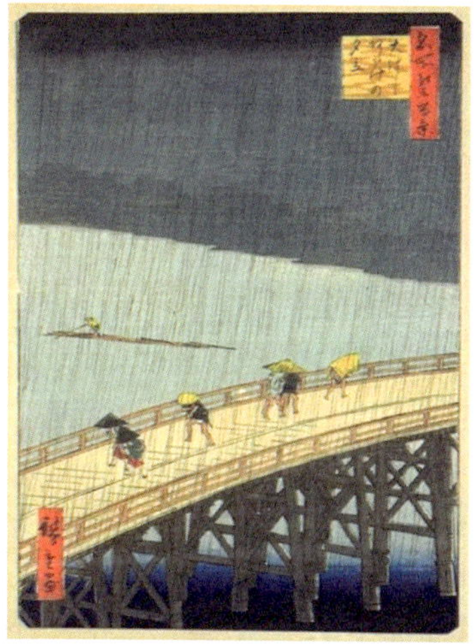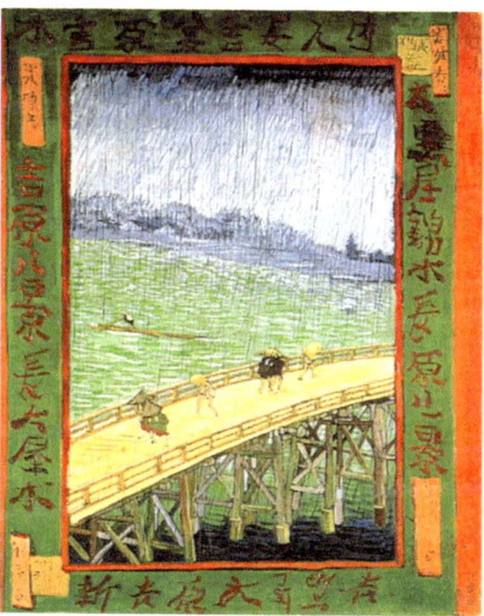

"Instead of trying to reproduce exactly what I see before me, I make more arbitrary use of color to express myself more forcefully. Well, let that be so—why should the painter not use every means to achieve expression as the poet does with words? (September 1888)

In contrast to Hiroshige's calmer mood—a sense of tranquility and a reflection of the Zen aesthetic—Van Gogh's lively color palette applied with thick expressive brushstrokes creates a more energetic and restless atmosphere, suitable to his signature style and psychological state. Hiroshige's meditative detachment now becomes a more expressive, felt experience of the landscape.

In Hiroshige's print, the boatman is nearly absorbed into the serenity of the calm water, blending seamlessly with the tranquil landscape. By contrast, Van Gogh intensifies the boatman's color, making him a commanding presence on the rippling blue-green water—a figure not lost into the scenery but boldly asserting himself within it. These changes reflect Van Gogh's personal engagement with nature, experienced not as something distant or sublime, but as something emotionally vibrant and alive.

Influenced by Hiroshige's perspective, the river flows in a diagonal line from light to the deepest velvety blue beneath the bridge. With the grey bridge support illuminated by splashes of mauve and maroon, the entire painting becomes a study in color.

Certainly, there is no blue without yellow and without orange, and if you put in the blue, then you must put in the yellow and orange as well (September 1888).

Heightening the color drama, the people crossing the yellow bridge streaked with orange and an orange railing add the essential hues. . . red green clothing, yellow straw hat, umbrella, and head covering. Framed with a vibrant red rim and red Japanese characters, this symphony of color is undeniably Van Gogh's. "It is not a mere copy, but rather an interpretation, my own way of seeing through their eyes."

The great Japanese ukiyo-e printmaker had a profound influence on him. In *Flowering Plum Orchard (after Hiroshige)* (1887), Van Gogh created his interpretation of Hiroshige's *Plum Garden at Kameido* transforming the orchard into his signature style.

Hiroshige's smooth, flat brushstrokes and subtle color palette are now bold and dynamic. Enhanced by the dark earthy tones of the tree trunks and branches, the white blossoms cradling yellow centers and the intense red-orange and golden ocher background now contrast dramatically with the cool dark green grass.

Like Hiroshige Van Gogh often depicted people in harmony with their surroundings. His strollers behind the fence—bolder, more vibrant tones set against a green background—lead the viewer's eye into the scene, their colorful garments—"as if they themselves are flowers"—suggest a deeper, more intimate relationship between humans and nature.

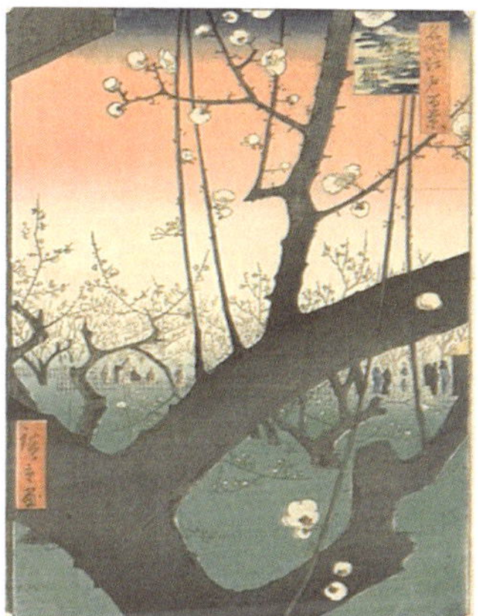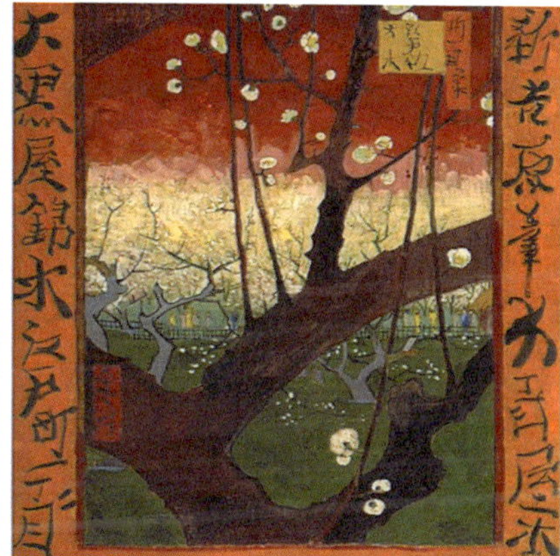

The Japanese live in nature as if they themselves are flowers; and that's how we should live as well—with nature and paintings (September 1888).

The Japanese characters around the painting bring honor to the spirit of the art he greatly admired. By removing the trees and fence and people, barely distinct, leaving only the vivid bands of color, both Japanese art and Van Gogh's interpretation clearly set a path for modern abstract artists to follow.

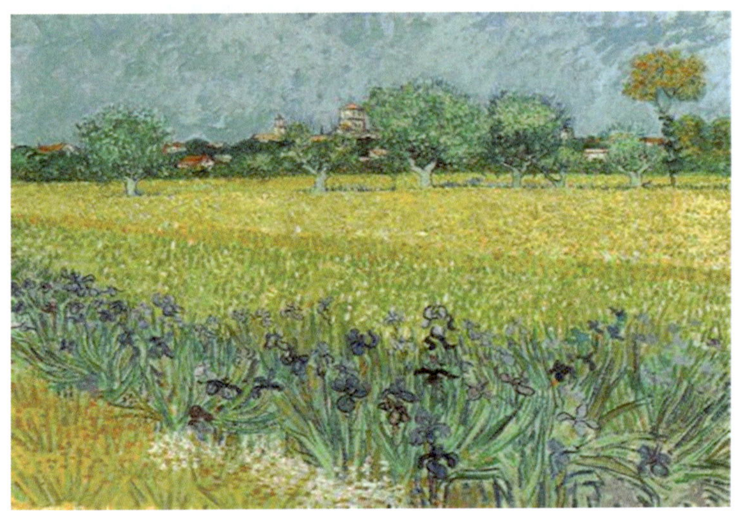

In *Fields with Irises near Arles* (1888) the bands of bold color are distinctly more obvious. Reflecting the Japanese emphasis on line, pattern, and essential form, the bold outlines and cropped framing of the irises—some cut off at the edge of the canvas—mirror the asymmetry and spontaneous viewpoints in ukiyo-e prints. All of which transform this simple landscape into a space of emotional contemplation and visual harmony, a simple image that captures the spirit of the place.

The quiet, expansive field evokes a sense of peaceful observation, much like the serene views of rivers, fields, and flowers in Japanese landscapes.

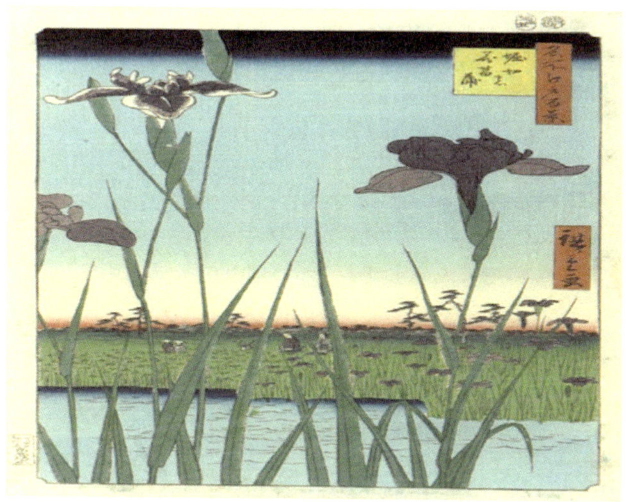

Hiroshige's *Irises at Horikiri*

Mark Rothko—and other Color Field painters—pushed the idea of emotional expression to its limits, stripping away recognizable forms entirely and using vast fields of color to evoke profound inner states. Rothko envisioned his paintings as secular altarpieces, spaces for meditation and existential reflection—silent encounters meant to stir the soul. In this, he echoes Van Gogh, who also saw painting as a deeply spiritual act. Both artists sought to move beyond surface appearances, using color to convey something eternal.

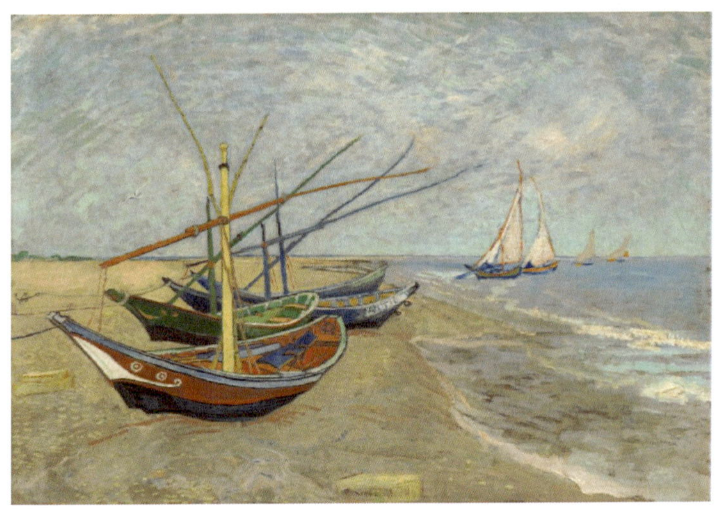

In *Fishing Boats on the Beach* at Saintes-Maries (1888), four boats stand out against the sand and sea. During periods of melancholy, nature, particularly the sea, had a restorative power for Van Gogh.

When one is in a somber mood, how good it is to walk on the barren beach and look at the grayish green water with the long white streaks of the waves (July 1883).

The Mediterranean has a colour like mackerel, in other words, changing—you don't always know if it's green or purple—you don't always know if it's blue—because a second later, its changing reflection has taken on a pink or grey hue . . . It's enchanting. The boats that are drawn up on the beach are colored like lobsters, green and red, and everything seems to have a kind of stylishness in the sunlight (June 1888).

His description of the sea "like mackerel," constantly shifting, inspired him to work with a palette of green and purple, blue, and pink and grey. The brilliant hues of the boats, standing out against the earthy tone of the sand, the light blueish-green sea, and swirling sky, create a warm and inviting scene.

Van Gogh studied his ukiyo-e prints with great care. The boats, sharply outlined, plainly echo the use of flat perspective, a significant Japanese influence on him and in the evolution of abstract art. But always the painting remains his own way of "seeing through their eyes." Here the flatness, slightly modified by the diagonal direction of the boats and the mast poles, add moderate depth to the scene. Inspired by the bold, simplified colors often seen in Japanese art, the bright blues, greens, and reds in the boats reflect Van Gogh's expressive use of color.

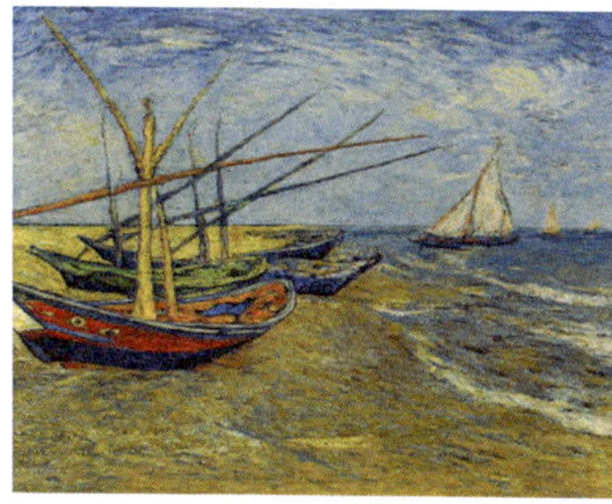 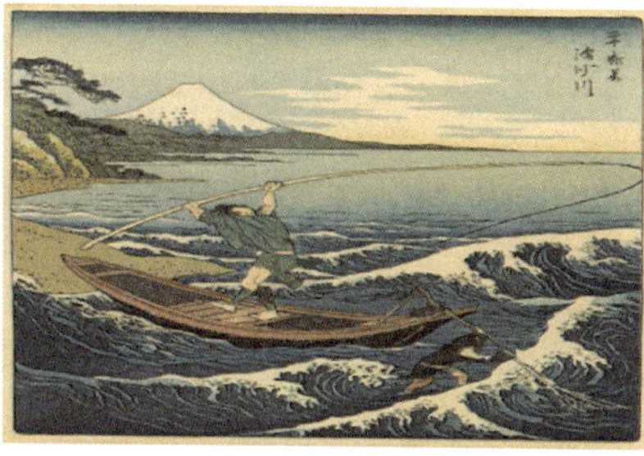

There is a striking resemblance between Van Gogh's painting and Hokusai's *Fishing Boats at Fukagawa.* A dominant horizontal element—the pole held by the boatman in Hokusai's print and the mast in Van Gogh's composition—sweeps from left to right, guiding the viewer's eye across the scene. The gentle curve of the rippling waves in Van Gogh's seascape and the triangular boat sails in the distance echo the fluid motion of the water and the iconic Mt. Fuji in Hokusai's work.

As a way of expressing *"how much joy"* he felt, Van Gogh painted *Almond Blossom* (1890), a gift for his newborn nephew. The flat plane of the turquoise-blue background, without heavy shading or depth, and the dark outlines around the branches and flowers flowing across the sky reflect the influence of the ukiyo-e prints.

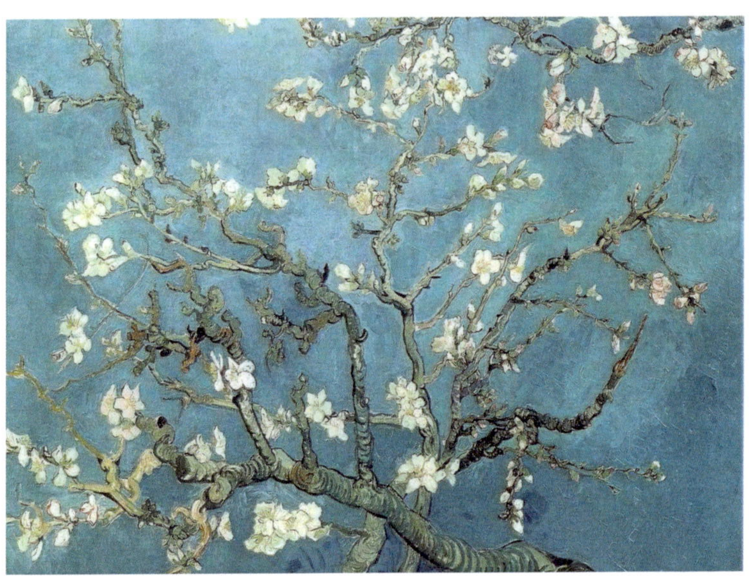

The buds and some petal edges are tinged with soft pinks and pale reds with just a hint of warm pink in the center of some blossoms, similar to the way plum blossoms grow. While the pink and reds are not dominant, their subtle presence adds depth and a whisper of warmth to the season's awakening. For Vincent the delicate floral imagery of the first flower to bloom in early spring symbolized not only the beauty in nature but also new life, love, and renewal.

I am working on a large canvas of almond trees in blossom, which I will send you soon It will be a piece of work for the birth of your son. . . I hope that looking at this canvas will bring a moment of calm, a little piece of happiness, like a branch of almond blossom against a blue sky... to remind you of the coming of spring, the renewal of life and of love, the tenderness we must carry within us . . . It's a way of expressing to you how much joy I feel for you . . . You'll see that it's perhaps the best, the most patiently worked thing I had done, painted with enthusiasm and with a heartbroken effort (February 1890).

Created with a "heartbroken effort, Vincent recently had been going through a very difficult emotional period in his life, the painting gave him a sense of "serenity" that he so desperately needed.

I would like to make paintings that express serenity, something like the way a cradle soothes (February 1890)

Irises 1889, painted in the garden at the Asylum, is considered one of his masterpieces. He frequently expressed how nature and flowers influenced his emotional state.

When I am well, I must pass months painting so as to recover what I have spent. The surroundings here are very beautiful, and there's something here that I find almost touching—a joy in the air, in the sun, and in everything, and it's so beautiful" (May 1889).

A single white iris set among deep purple and blue irises boldly contrasting with the bright green leaves and yellow-orange earth creates a dynamic emotional intensity—that "joy in the air."

For it's a beautiful study of the yellow, the blue, the various greens (September 1889).

Unlike traditional Western art, which often relied on shading and linear perspective, Van Gogh's use of flattened spatial design—characteristic of ukiyo-e prints—conveys depth through layering and rhythmic line. The overlapping forms, cropped

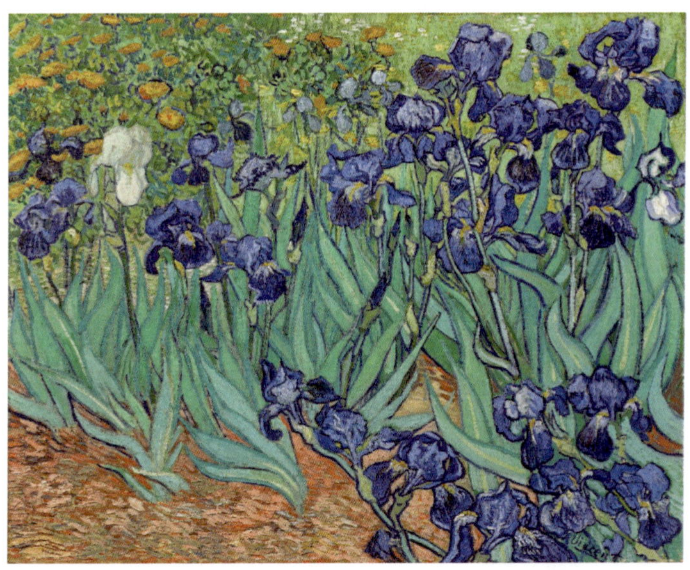

edges, and fluid outlines—especially the bold contours around flowers, twisting leaves, and stems—clearly reflect the influence of Japanese art.

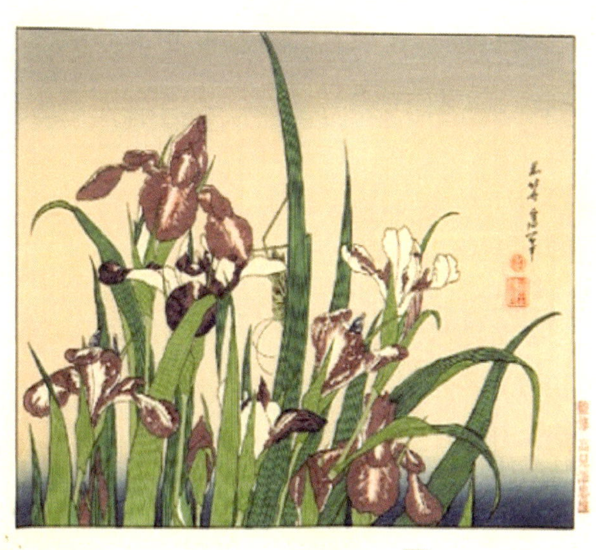

Hiroshige's Irises and Butterfly.

The vibrant palette and expressive, swirling brushstrokes breathe life into Van Gogh's irises, capturing not only their physical beauty but also their transient vitality. In various stages—budding, blooming, and withering—the flowers embody

the fleeting nature of existence. This quiet evocation of impermanence reflects the spirit of *mono no aware*, the Japanese aesthetic
of the melancholic awareness of both the beauty and the transience of the season.

*There is something infinitely healing in the repeated refrains of
nature—the assurance that dawn comes after night, and spring after winter (October 1882).*

Langlois Bridge at Arles with Women Washing (1888) evoked
a strong sense of home for Van Gogh. Painted in Arles shortly after his arrival in the south of France in early 1888, the drawbridge
and canal reminded him of the drawbridges in The Netherlands,
especially those near his childhood home in Zundert and later in
Nuenen and The Hague. He chose Arles as a retreat from Paris
and the pressures of urban life. The bridge, with its tranquil canal
and open space, became a symbol of the calm, ordered beauty he
was seeking in the south of France.

The painting clearly serves as a compelling homage to the
spirit of Hokusai's *The Drum Bridge at Meguro and Sunse (1830-
1832).* Both artists create a calm, stable composition of a peaceful scene with details of daily life. Van Gogh's women washing
laundry by the edge of the canal reaffirm his respect for rural life
and labor. Although the women are not the central subject—a
quiet moment of rural life held firm in color and form—they
are a natural part of the scenery and blend seamlessly into the
landscape, much like in Japanese prints. Hokusai's boatman, fish-
erman and figures strolling across the bridge capture the quiet
rhythm in the soft light at sunset of a pleasant day by the water.
Both scenes evoke the poetic in the prosaic, a transient moment
that will endure in the heart of the viewer.

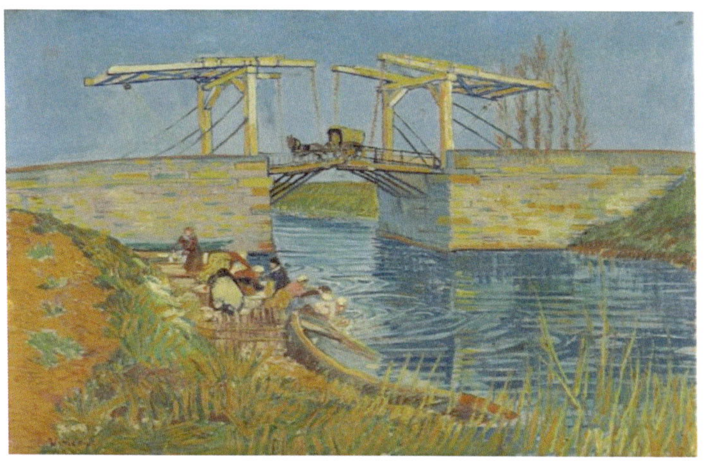

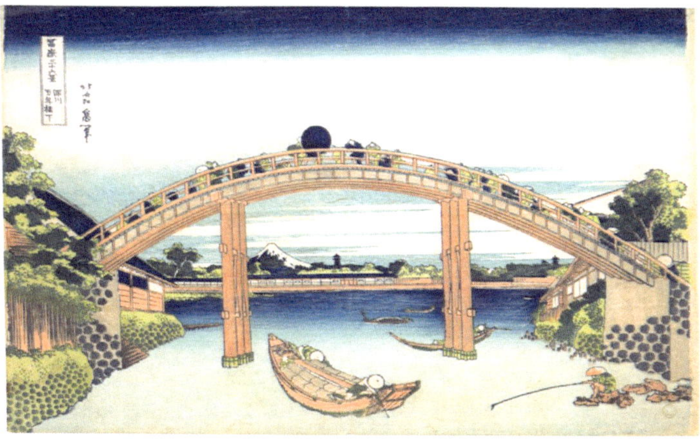

Unlike the Renaissance tradition of Western art, which emphasized realism through linear perspective and chiaroscuro, Hokusai's flattened space, strong contour lines, and harmonious colors influenced Van Gogh's choice of a flattened color field enhanced by bold outlines around the bridge, the women, and the boat. Although his brushstrokes—shorter, flatter, and more controlled than usual—reflect the influence of Japanese prints, they remain true to his expressive style, emphasizing texture and movement. The water is not a mirror but a surface alive. The emphasis is on pattern. The soft, luminous color palette—the clear blue sky, the warm ochers of the bridge, and the soft greens of the riverbanks—creates an anchor of calm. Evoking this quiet moment in a single day—an affirmation of a memory of his childhood home and a hope for a new life in a tranquil landscape in Arles—gave Van Gogh the peace he so desperately needed

Japanese art, with its clarity, its marvelous sense of composition, and its economy of means, is a refreshing influence—it clears the brain, it refines the mind (September 1888).

Van Gogh lived in The Hague from late 1880 until 1883. The flat, expansive, low-lying land characterized by canals, meadows, and pollarded willows influenced his painting at this time. In *Pollard Willow* 1882 Van Gogh turns a simple Dutch meadow tree into a powerful image of solitude and bleak beauty.

I've attacked that old giant of a pollard willow . . . a sombre landscape . . . a sky with scudding clouds. . . I believe it has turned out the best of the watercolours. . . where the black is darkest in this little

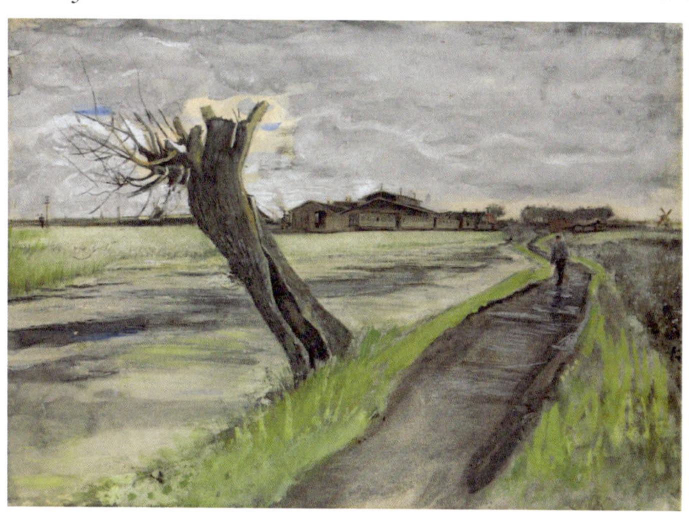

sketch is where the greatest strengths are in the watercolur – dark green, brown, dark grey (July 1882.)

Traditionally willow trees are associated with melancholy, resilience, and regeneration—a poignant meditation on the cycle of life, death, and renewal. In *Pollard Willow*, the "hushed" willow anchored in the "glow" of smoothly "scudding clouds," its harshly pruned crown haloed in soft washes of white, blue, and pink creates a deeply stirring image of wounded beauty. When paired with Van Gogh's own words, the haunting image becomes emotionally charged.

They are like tired old beggars, the willows, their heads bowed down. Or like old grandfathers—one can't help thinking of certain human figures when one sees them (October 1882).

The tree as a suffering man reflects Van Gogh's early transition from social realism to symbolic expression. As he progressed in this style, he wrote,

In the end, I do not invent the whole picture. On the contrary, I find it already in nature—I just have to disentangle it (May 1888).

And disentangle he did—transforming what he saw into a deeply personal vision. The naturalistic, yet somber earth tones—browns, greens, and grays—evoke the stark, damp Dutch winter landscape, reinforcing a mood of desolation. The lone figure traveling down a quiet road mirrors Van Gogh's melancholic, introspective state during this early and difficult period of his life. Struggling both financially and emotionally and deeply troubled with his progress as an artist, this solitary willow becomes a symbol of quiet strength in adversity—an expression of his inner turmoil. His relationship with the world around him was always intensely intimate and profoundly personal.

The year 1888 marks the beginning of a very difficult period in Van Gogh's life, a long period of mental illness. *A View of Arles* (1888), an uncommon view in Japanese perspective, painted during this time reflects his desire to heal.

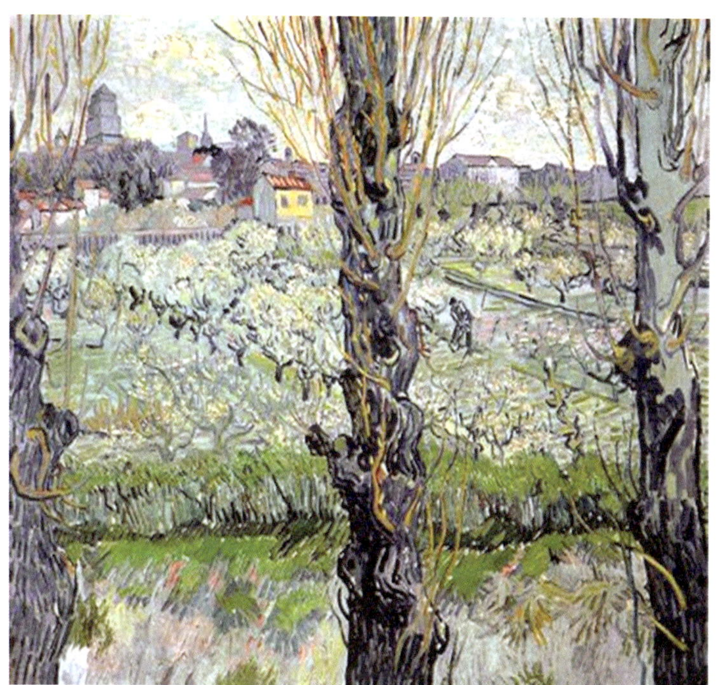

Viewed through three large cropped gnarled tree trunks in the foreground, a field of wintry greens sprout shoots of spring. Created shortly before he committed himself to Saint Paul de Mausole, the asylum at St. Remy, the painting reveals Vincent's struggle with mental illness and feelings of solitude at this time. The tree trunks, foreshadowing the bars of the asylum cell at St. Remy, express a personal sense of isolation. Refusing to give into his feelings of loneliness, he wrote to his brother,

I just finished a painting of a view of Arles, with the gnarled tree trunks and fields so characteristic of the place . . . These gnarled tree trunks seem to suggest strength and a certain roughness which I find particularly moving (October 1888).

Nature—both inspiring and healing—intercedes and encourages Van Gogh to carry on despite his pain. Amid the light and pale color, the lone figure turns the soil, emphasizing a union between humanity and nature, a comforting connection that Van Gogh deeply yearned for. The softer hues evoke a serene mood and a quiet hope for new life and regeneration. With the coming of spring, the tilling of the soil, and the church spire in the distance, the entire scene becomes a meditation on renewal for the earth, for humanity, and for Vincent.

Van Gogh painted *The Courtyard of the Hospital at Arles* (1889) while recovering from his mental breakdown

Its arcaded gallery like in Arab buildings, whitewashed in front of these galleries, an ancient garden with a pond in the middle and 8 beds of flowers, forget-me-nots, Christmas roses, anemones, buttercups, sunflowers, daisies. And beneath the gallery, orange trees and oleanders. So it's a painting chock-full of flowers and springtime greenery. However, three black, sad trees cross it like snakes, and in the foreground four large sad, dark box bushes (April 1889).

Although the dynamic color contrasts create an environment conducive to recovery—nature as a place of solace—the flowers and greenery are enclosed by "three black, sad trees" crossing it "like snakes" and "four sad, dark box bushes" in the foreground offering an intimate view into Van Gogh's psychological state at this time The natural world had become a vessel for his personal struggles. The energetic brushstrokes, particularly in the "sad, dark box bushes," convey this emotional intensity. In one of the most difficult periods in his short life, the painting becomes a powerful expression of a soul in turmoil.

Anne Dupré

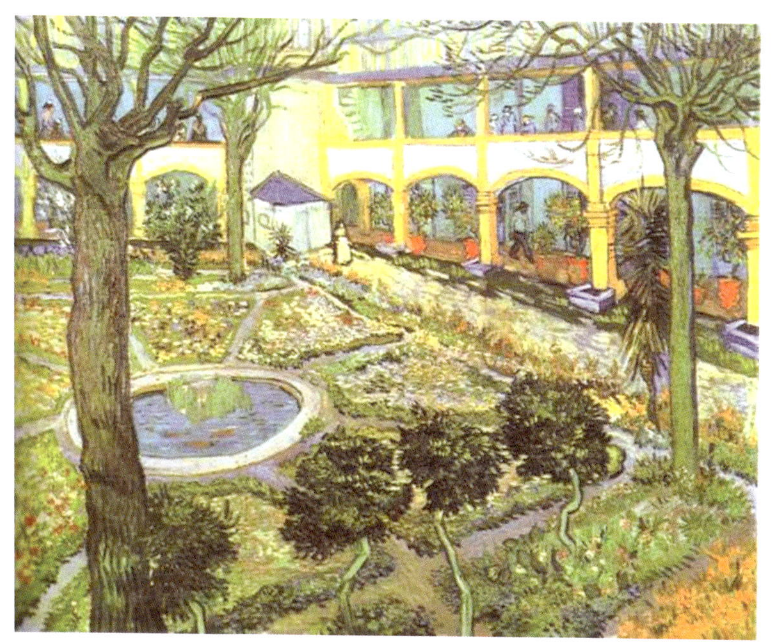

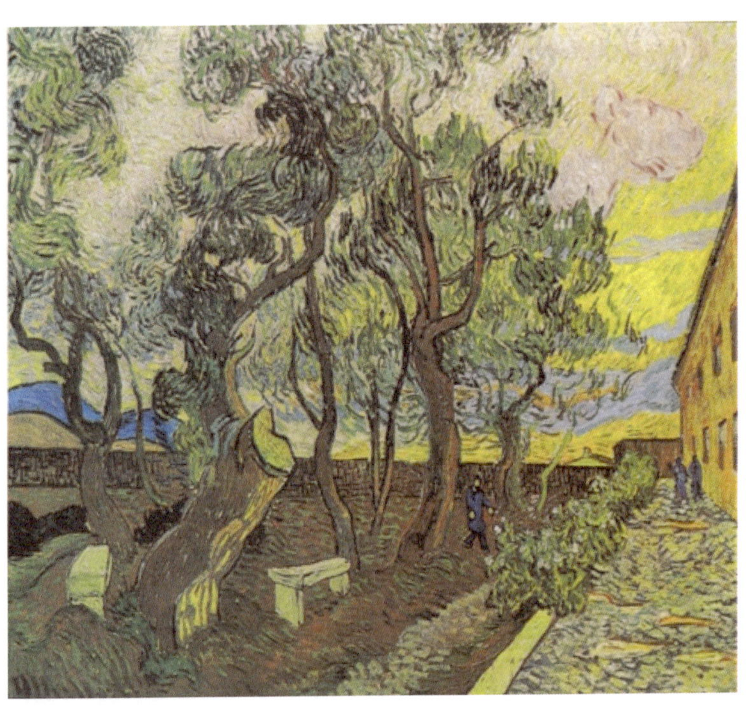

I find them full of soul, like those who have suffered yet endure.

In 1889 Van Gogh's stay at Saint-Paul de Mausole, the psychiatric institution in Saint-Remy de Provence, was both painful and productive—he created around 150 of his most important paintings. In these final, turbulent years of his life, he infused many of his works with a deep emotional and spiritual connection to nature. This profound bond can clearly be seen in his series of olive tree paintings, where he not only explored their natural beauty but also their complex relationship to humanity—and to his own inner struggles.

The olive trees with the white flowers around them are something I have worked on a lot (November 1889).

Writing to his brother Theo, he described *Olive Trees in the Garden of Saint Paul's Hospital* (1889) in vivid, almost poetic terms.

These tall trees stand out against an evening sky streaked with violet against a yellow background. High up, the yellow turns to pink, turns to green. A wall – red ocher again – blocks the view, and there's nothing above it but a violet and yellow ocher hill. Now, the first tree is an enormous trunk, but struck by lightning and sawn off. A side branch, thrusts up very high, however, and falls down again in an avalanche of dark green twigs. This dark giant – like a proud man brought low – contrasts, when seen as the character of a living being, with the pale smile of the last rose on the bush, which is fading in front of him. Under the trees, empty stone benches, dark box. The sky is reflected yellow in a puddle after the rain. A ray of sun - the last glimmer - exalts the dark ocher to orange - small dark figures prowl here and there between the trunks. You'll understand that this combination of red ocher, of green saddened with gray, of black lines that define the outlines, this gives rise a little that feeling of anxiety from which some of my companions in misfortune often suffer and which is called "seeing red". And what's more, the motif of the great tree struck by lightning, the sickly pink and green smile of the last flower of autumn, confirms this idea (October 1889).

In his efforts to capture "the anxiety from which some of his companions in misfortune often suffer," he has undoubtedly revealed his own inner pain.

The olive trees are very characteristic, and I am struggling to catch their essence. Sometimes they seem to be old silver, other times green and bronze, their twisted trunks and gnarled forms showing their age and struggle. I find them full of soul, like those who have suffered yet endure (October 1889).

Aurier observed that Van Gogh's "trees, twisted like giants in battle, proclaiming with the gestures of their gnarled menacing arms and with the tragic waving of their green manes, their indomitable power, the pride of their musculature, their blood-hot sap, their eternal defiance of hurricane, lightning, and malevolent Nature."

Standing "twisted like giants in battle," the olive trees, rich in texture and color and "full of soul, like those who have suffered yet endure" remain a psychological study of Van Gogh's own pain.

The interplay of movement and color, the sky a turbulent striated mix of blue and bright yellow and pink in contrast to the soil's warm earth tones, enhance the emotional intensity. The three figures in the distance, somewhat indistinct and insignificant, reflect Van Gogh's own feelings of separation from society and the patients at the Asylum.

Although Van Gogh's severed tree trunk in the foreground expresses impermanence—that fleeting moment in the cycle of life—it still stands. And like the tree, Vincent remains "full of soul" in his will to paint the very best he could. Providing consolation and quiet strength, his olive trees poignantly embody the enduring tension between hope and suffering.

The bold black outlined trees, flat unshaded planes of color, and asymmetrical perspective reflect the influence of Japanese woodblock prints. The elegant curvature of the trees and trunks of Hiroshige's *The Pine Grove of Miho in Suruga Province* created a clear path for him to follow. Yet Van Gogh did not imitate Japanese art—he translated it into his own deeply personal and expressive vision.

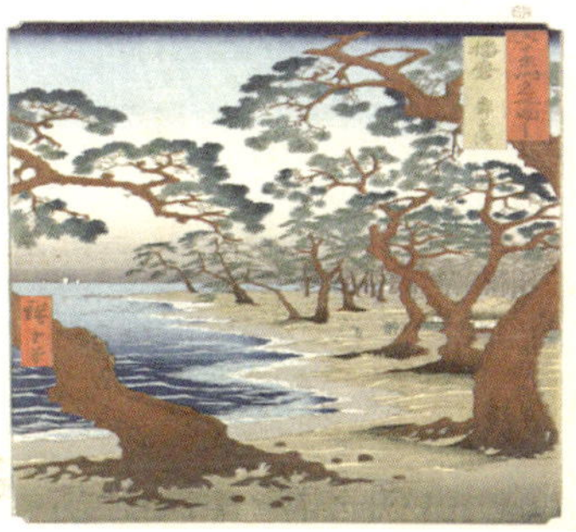 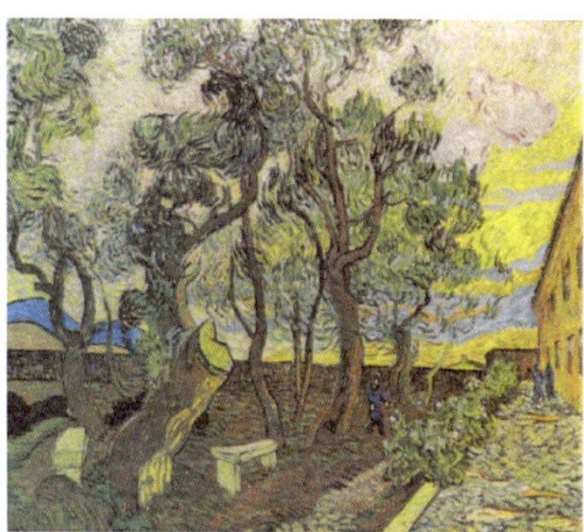

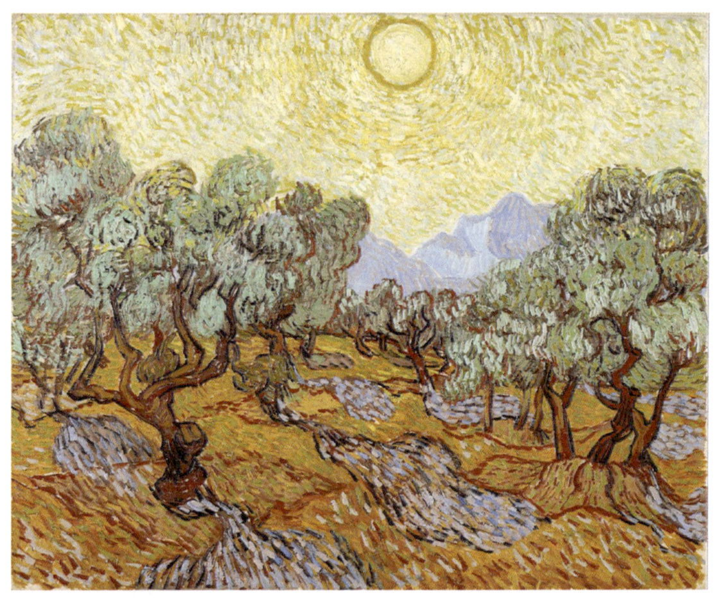

In Olive Trees (1889) the gnarled and twisted forms express a sense of struggle but also a feeling of renewal as their beauty continues to change through the seasons.

The olive tree is something else; it is more Greek. It's a fine sight to see them standing there . . . grey-green against the yellow soil . . . The effect of it is very lively and full of poetry, (June 1889).

The olive tree . . . if you want to compare it to something, something like the figure of a Michelangelo – rugged, gnarled, twisted. But more than that, it speaks of the eternal – it is symbolic to me, especially after reading the Gospels – the Mount of Olives, where Christ suffered (November 1889).

The bold brushstrokes, the vibrant color palette, the power of the sun's life-giving energy express a deep emotional and spiritual response. Through vivid colors and symbolic subject matter, Van Gogh transforms a natural scene into a powerful message of his personal spirituality.

Women Picking Olives 1889 becomes a symbolic expression of the harmony between humanity and nature.

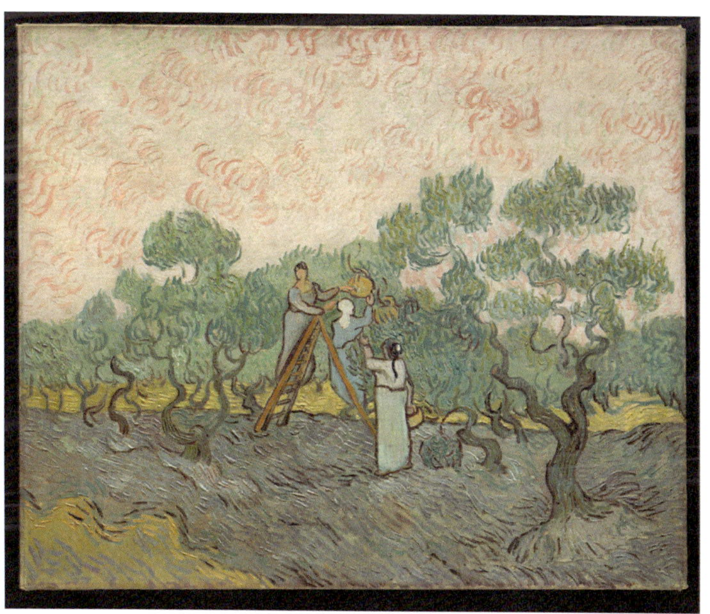

I shall not paint a Christ in the Garden of Olives, but shall paint the olive harvest as one might see it today, and by giving human figure its proper place in it, one might perhaps be reminded of it all the same. (November 1889).

The olive tree(s) is something which speaks to me of the Christ, a symbol of his agony—it is not the garden in its appearance, but in its emotion that I see it (December 1889).

Emile Bernard, a young artist friend, began to develop theoretical ideas that diverged from Van Gogh's expressive realism. In a letter to Bernard, Vincent wrote,

I am telling you that one can give an impression of anguish, without aiming straight at the historic garden of Gethsemane; that it is not necessary to portray the characters of the Sermon on the Mount in order to produce a consoling and gentle motif (March 1888).

Echoing Gethsemane and spiritual anguish, Van Gogh's olive trees are "full of soul."

In capturing a street scene where he lived in *A Pork-Butcher's Shop Seen From a Window* (1888), Vincent presents another unconventional view of Japanese perspective. From the slightly elevated vantage point, both the viewer and the figure at the window can look down onto the street and store front below—a hallmark of ukiyo-e prints, where the perspective is tilted from above rather than at eye level, as seen in the works of Hiroshige and Hokusai.

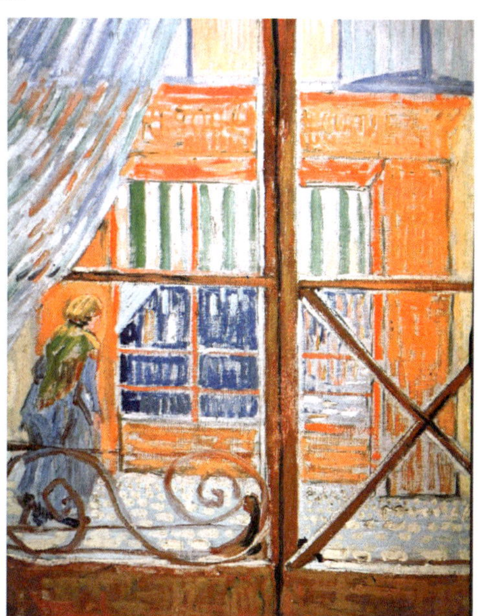

Looking out at the world one may have a great fire inside, and yet no one comes to sit by it. Passerby see only a wisp of smoke and continue on their way (July 1880).

The swirling energetic brushstrokes, bold colors, and thick application of paint create a sense of movement—a sense of life moving on, moving forward without him. "Looking out at the world" passing by from an enclosure expresses Vincent's profound feeling of solitude and reaffirms his determination to paint the best that he was capable of doing.

What am I in the eyes of most people? A nonentity or an eccentric and disagreeable man—someone who has no position in society and never will have, in short, the lowest of the low. Very well, then—if that were absolutely true, then I should like to show by my work what there is in the heart of such an eccentric, such a nobody (July 1882).

His ability to inject feelings of his personal struggles into the most commonplace settings makes his art so universally resonant.

At Eternity's Gate (1890) was based on an earlier lithograph entitled *Worn Out* (1882) inspired by real-life observations of a man at a poorhouse in The Hague. In 1890 Van Gogh returned to this subject just weeks before the end of his life, The painting –a profoundly human image of a man bowed down in loneliness and despair, his face buried in his hands—resonates deeply with Van Gogh's own personal feelings.

I feel –a failure. That's it as regards me—I feel that this is the destiny that I accept, that I will never change. Yet in the face of that, and in the face of grief that cannot be spoken, I go on painting (July 1890).

While the man in *At Eternity's Gate* does not resemble Van Gogh physically, the emotional intensity and symbolic posture make it widely interpreted as a profound emotional self-portrait. Art historians see it as a deeply personal expression of loneliness, fatigue, and spiritual anguish near the end of his life.

This stripped-down portrayal of loneliness and despair is Van Gogh's final meditation on the fragility of the human spirit, capturing with haunting simplicity the emotional vulnerability, existential exhaustion, and spiritual turmoil that defined his final months. The bowed posture, muted tones, and stark setting condense a lifetime of suffering into a single, heartfelt image that speaks not only to Van Gogh's personal anguish but to the uni-

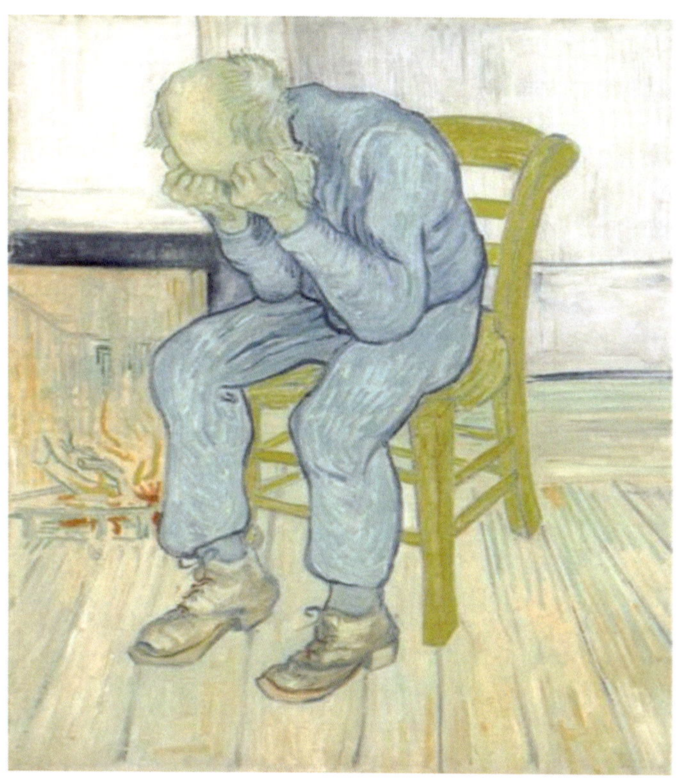

versal human experience of grief, isolation, and the search for meaning at the end of life.

As the title suggests the man is at the threshold of death contemplating the vast unknown. If you accept that Van Gogh sees himself in this image, it clearly aligns with his struggle to reconcile his faith and suffering with what lies ahead. Despite the overwhelming despair, the title doesn't close the door—it places the man at the gate of eternity, giving him hope and leaving him room for redemption.

But the soul of the person. . . must be in the eyes

Unwavering in his admiration for Japanese art, Van Gogh depicted himself as a Buddhist monk in *Self-Portrait as a Bonze Dedicated to Gauguin* (1888). His calm demeanor evokes the meditative qualities of a Buddhist monk.

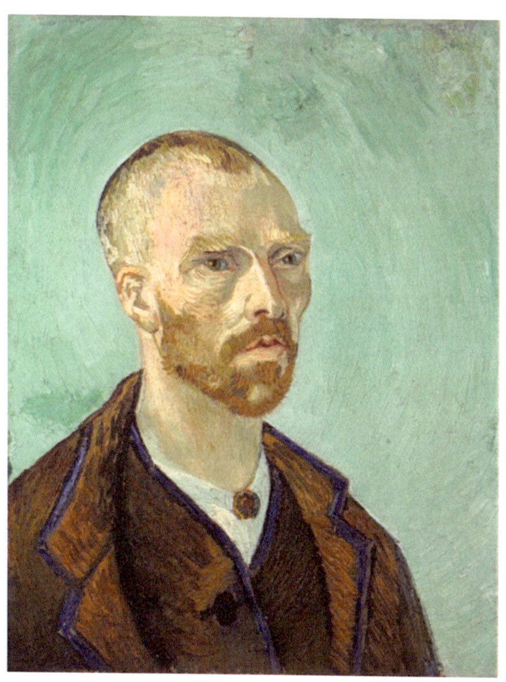

Meyer Shapiro wrote, "In Van Gogh, for the first time in the history of art, the painter becomes the main subject of his painting. The artist is no longer a neutral observer, but someone who transforms what he sees into a deeply personal vision."

Created during a critical period in his life when he was seeking inner peace, the portrait, a spiritual and psychological drama, reveals his deep immersion into Japanese art and philosophy.

I have a portrait of myself, all ash-colored . . . But as I also exaggerate my personality I have in the first place aimed at the character of a simple bonze worshiping the Eternal Buddha (September 1884).

Vincent held Japanese artists in high esteem, admiring their communal spirit and harmonious way of life—much like that of a Buddhist monk. In his portrait, he strove to embody the serene and contemplative qualities he associated with their Bonze portraits. Hoping to escape the mental turmoil he was experiencing, he turned inward through his art, creating an image that is at once spiritual, introspective, and quietly resolute.

The flat background and sharp contours reflect the influence of ukiyo-e woodblock prints.

"Portrait of Hokusai" by Keisai Eisen, a renown Japanese Ukiyo-e artist.

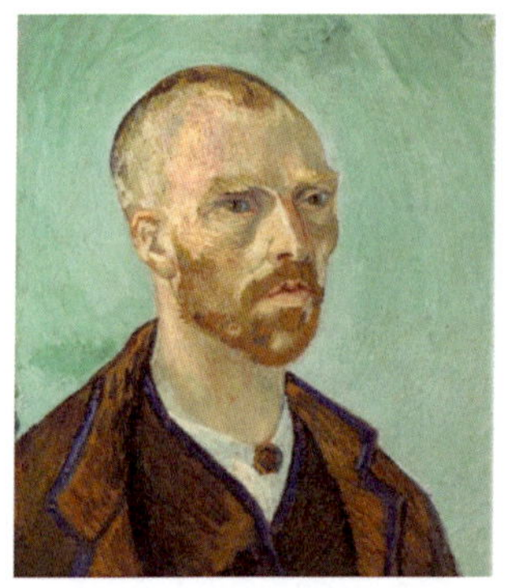
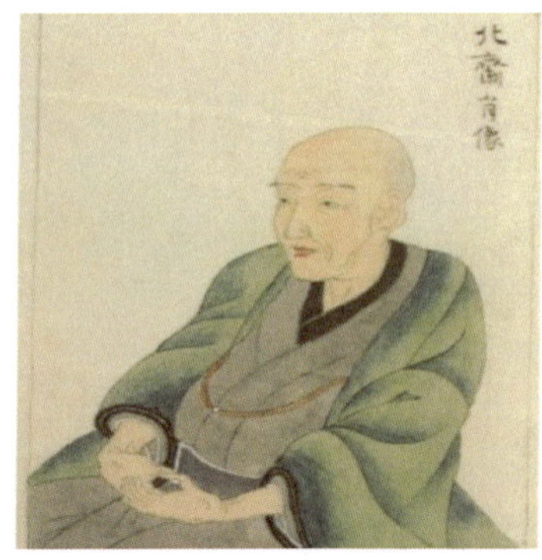

You will see, I hope, that in my portrait I have painted the dull ocher and sad green of the Japanese Bonzes. . . (September 1888).

The shaved head and ascetic appearance suggest a correlation between Van Gogh's suffering and the self-discipline of a monk. Although not clearly defined, the amulet around his neck closely resembles a Buddhist talisman or rosary symbolizing spiritual protection or meditation.

I'm looking for a deeper likeness than that obtained by a photographer. People say, and I am willing to believe it, that it is hard to know oneself—but it is also difficult to paint oneself. The eyes, the mouth, the neck—are always difficult. But the soul of the person—if it is to be shown—must be in the eyes (July 1888).

His introspective gaze expresses self-reflection, and the contemplative mood, subtly unsettled by the use of dull ocher and "sad" green tones on his gaunt face, evokes a quiet tension between spiritual calm and inner unrest The red beard and hair, a color usually associated with strong emotion and often symbolic of passion and intensity, suggest the fiery temperament of a spirit in torment. Seeing himself as an ascetic devoted to something greater than himself gave him the will to persevere in spite of his pain.

Ah well, I think of myself as a simple bonze in a temple, seated in front of a picture, and I would like to dedicate my whole life to painting. . . (September 1888).

Stripped of vanity and exposing his suffering in *Portrait with a Bandaged Ear (1889)*, Van Gogh creates an intimate view of his fragile mental state during this difficult period in his life—the infamous ear-cutting incident.

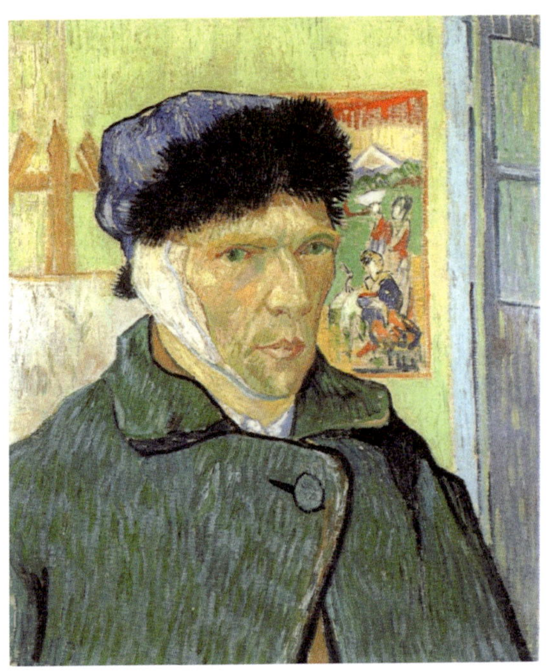

The act of painting still gives me strength, and though I am alone much of the time, I do not feel lost when I have the canvas before me. I hope this portrait will tell you more than I can say. It is not only a picture of my likeness but also a reflection of my state—troubled, perhaps, yet still striving toward something true (January 1889).

His steady gaze reveals not only an intense emotional unrest but a fierce determination to keep painting—" troubled, perhaps, yet still striving toward something true." Although characterized by his signature use of color, the palette, greenish-yellow tones contrasting with the cool blue of his hat and darker green coat, is somewhat muted, a reflection of his subdued mood and critical emotional state. His gaunt face, tight lips, and tired, sorrowful eyes convey pain and isolation.

In the background to the right is a clear homage to Hiroshige. Even in this difficult moment of mental distress, Van Gogh includes a quiet tribute to one of the Japanese artists he deeply admired—an affirmation of beauty and order amid his personal turmoil. Painting was his passion, a way of expressing his emotions, and often his only source of solace.

In *The Peasant (Patience Escalier* 1888) Van Gogh creates a striking portrait of a hardworking gardener and former cowherd. Inspired by the works of Jean-Francois Millet whom he consid-

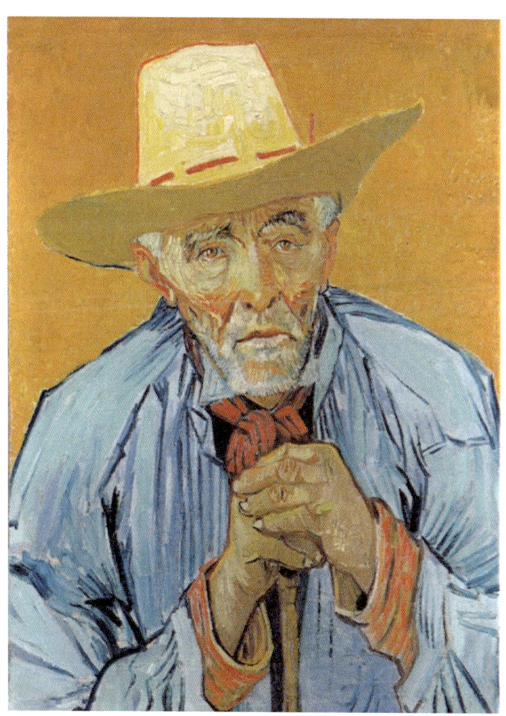

ered a pioneering figure in depicting peasants and workers that embody the soul and the dignity of rural life, he wrote,

Millet is father Millet, the eternal soul of peasant life. . . I have just finished a portrait of a peasant, a study like the one of the Postman, but more severe. It is an old peasant, a man who resembles a worn-out old horse—who has plowed a lot of furrows in the earth. A bright orange background, blue clothes, and a tanned, sun-drenched face. Ah, how I long to make portraits that express something other than a mere resemblance! ... I want to paint men and women with that something of the eternal which the halo used to symbolize, and which we seek to convey by the very radiance and vibration of our colors (August 1888).

The thick brushstrokes, Van Gogh's signature style in his later works, enhance the roughness of the peasant's skin, indicating years of hard labor in the sun. His weathered hands, folded front and center as if in prayer, and the yellow brimmed straw much like a padre priest hat give him "that something of the eternal," reinforcing the dignity and even divinity in the peasant's life of physical labor.

His face—especially the weary solemn eyes—suggests endurance. But the bold, vibrant warm palette belies his weariness. The earthy tone of his face and hands, the bright yellow hat, and the sun-kissed orange background contrasting with his striking blue coat capture the soul of the peasant and give the portrait emotional depth, that something of the "eternal" through the very "radiance and vibration" of color.

In Van Gogh's eyes, Eugene Boch, a friend and an artist, had "a Dante-like face".

I very much like the looks of this young man with his distinctive face, like the blade of grass. . . and distinction with all that (July 1888).

In *The Poet (Portrait of Eugene Boch)* 1888, Van Gogh strove to capture someone who sees beauty and truth beyond the sur-

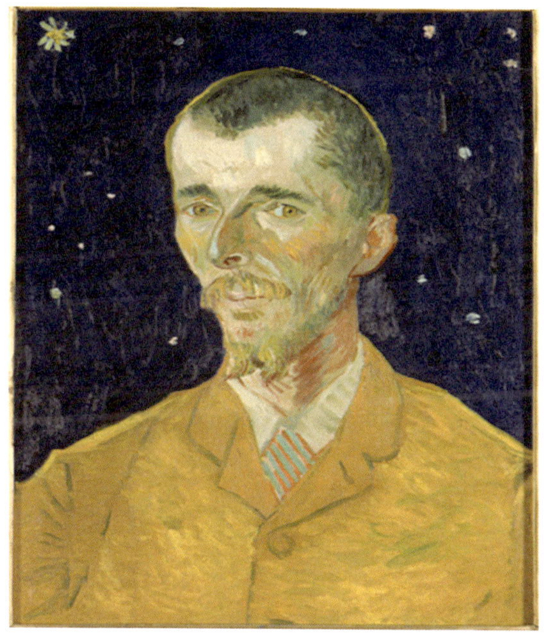

face, a man with a poetic vision *who dreams great dreams*

I should like to paint the portrait of an artist friend, a man who dreams great dreams, who works as the nightingale sings, because it is his nature... To paint a man's portrait, I must paint his dreams too... I do not want to achieve realism, but something deeper, something that captures his soul. That is why I am doing his portrait, not in an ordinary background, but in the setting of a starry night. Because he is a poet, and poetry is written in the stars (August 1888).

He admired Thomas Carlyle who became the light in his path. The Poet as "a man who dreams great dreams" was derived from Carlyle's *On Heroes, Hero-Worship, and the Heroic in History.* Carlyle wrote,

"The Poet (Artist) is a seer; a gift of vision has been given to him. He is the man of the whole world, in all ages, who first perceives and foretells it; who sees, through all entanglements, the truth of things; the great soul, open to the Divine Significance of Life. If you consider it, what is a Poet but a Prophet asleep in his dreams?"

In these words, Van Gogh recognized his own struggles and aspirations—a calling to create beauty from suffering and to elevate the soul through art. Rendered in delicate brushstrokes and vibrant tones, dominated by warm yellows and oranges, Van Gogh's idealized vision of the poet as a dreamer becomes a reality. The stillness in his face and his eyes, lost in thought, give him a gentle, almost ethereal presence.

By setting a light-colored face against a dark background, I try to express the thoughts of a face... Instead of trying to reproduce exactly what I have before my eyes, I use color more arbitrarily in order to express myself forcibly. (Letter to his sister September 1888).

The "light-colored face against a dark background" highlights the subject's inner world.

Behind his head, instead of painting the ordinary wall of this shabby apartment, I will paint infinity, I will do a simple background of the richest blue, the most intense blue that I can create, and through this simple combination of the bright head against this rich, blue background, I will obtain a mysterious effect, like a star in the depths of an azure sky (October,1888).

All of Van Gogh's portraits reveal profound psychological depth. The *Portrait of Dr. Gachet (1890)* painted just weeks before Van Gogh's death was one of the most emotionally charged and is now considered one of the most celebrated works of his final period

I have seen Dr. Gachet, who gives me the impression of being rather eccentric, but his experience as a doctor must keep him balanced and firm. He is much more nervous and much he speaks of her constantly. I have found a true friend in him, something like another brother—it comforts me enormously" (May 1890).

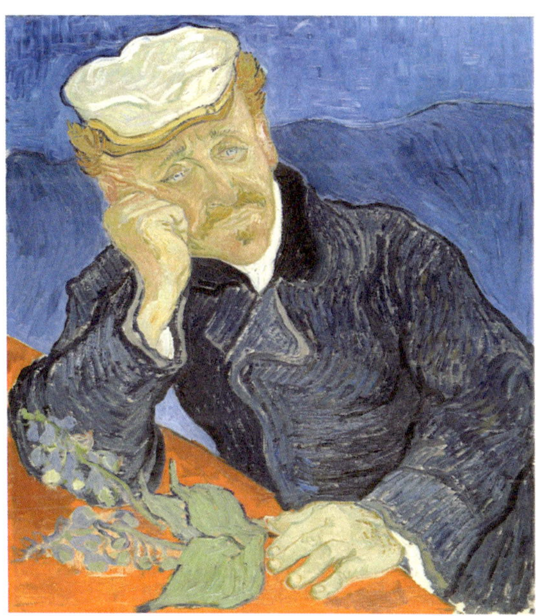

The homeopathic physician, who cared for Van Gogh in Auvers during the final months of his life, appears tired and deeply introspective.

I have a portrait of Dr. Gachet with the heartbroken expression of our time. . . The day I painted Dr. Gachet I gave him an expression of melancholy that might look like a grimace to many who

see the canvas. But it's necessary to paint this way; otherwise, one cannot grasp how, compared to the serenity of old portraits, modern faces are filled with expression and passion—like they are waiting for something, still growing (June 1890).

The foxglove on the table before him is a homeopathic heart medication but also an herb rich in symbolism—often associated with foreshadowing death. Enhanced by the blues, the purples, and the greens which heighten the melancholic mood, Dr. Gachet's down cast eyes and slumped posture express despair.

Completed just a few weeks before Van Gogh died, the painting expresses his efforts to depict shared suffering through his art. "He is a true friend, something like another brother"—a brother in pain, and a mirror of Van Gogh's own deeply emotional state at this time.

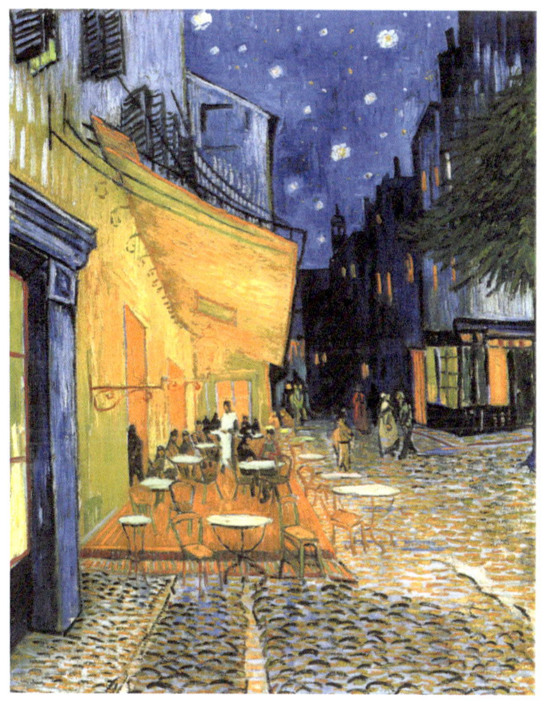

Cafe Terrace at Night (1888), a harmonious and vibrant blend
of blues and yellows and oranges, captures the warmth of an out-
door scene on a pleasant starry night. Vincent wrote to his sister,

Now there's a painting of night without black. With nothing but beautiful blue and violet and green, and in this you'll see the square lit with gaslight and the pink glow of the café. And a starry blue sky—and violet-blue houses. It's painted from life, on the spot... (September 1888).

The illumination from the gaslight contrasts beautifully with the haloed stars swirling in the deep purple and blue night sky. The perspective as your eye moves from the cobblestone street, past the glowing terrace to the star-filled night sky creates a strong sense of depth.

Highlighting Van Gogh's signature impasto, the dynamic and varied application of paint in the cool blue sky, the circular strokes haloing the stars, and the short, choppy strokes on the warm yellow-orange café generate a sense of movement. Although Van Gogh focuses more on the atmosphere, the figures barely defined appear sociable, their presence creates a warm and inviting social scene under the canopy of haloed stars in the rich blue sky. Life moves on at a comfortable and peaceful pace—all too rare in Van Gogh's oeuvre.

Standing apart from many of his more emotionally turbulent works, this painting was done during a relatively stable period in his life. He had moved to Arles in the south of France with hopes of starting an artist's community and was deeply inspired by the light, colors, and landscapes of the region. For a brief time, he felt hopeful.

In contrast, *The Night Café* (1888), painted during his long solitary nights of insomnia in Arles, is a haunting depiction of the interior of a late-night café. The jarring colors and distorted perspective create an intense emotional atmosphere evoking despair.

I have tried to express the terrible passions of humanity by means of red and green. The room is blood red and dull yellow, with a green billiard table in the middle, four lemon yellow lamps with a glow of orange and green. Everywhere it is a battle and antithesis of the most different reds and greens, in the figures of the little sleeping hooligans, in the empty dreary room, in the violet and blue. . . I have tried to express the idea that the café is a place where one can ruin oneself, go mad, or commit a crime. I have tried to express the power of darkness in a low public house by soft Louis XV green and Malachite, contrasting with the yellow greens and harsh blue greens, and all this in an atmosphere like a devil's furnace, in pale sulphur (September 1888).

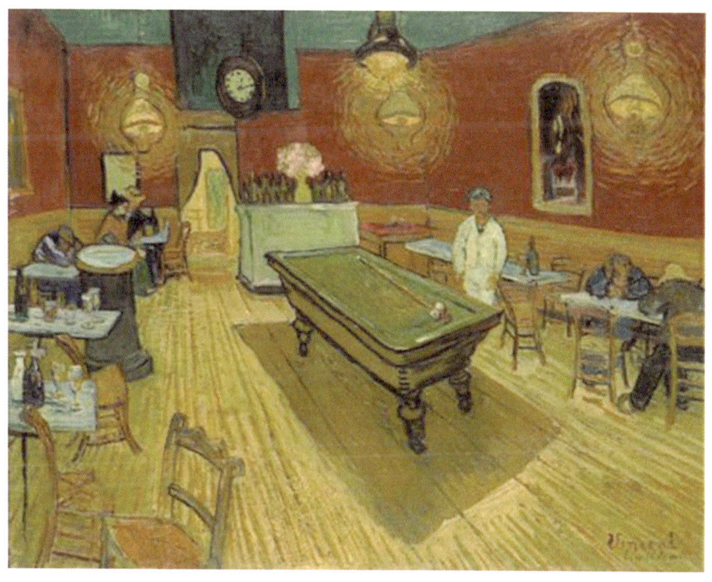

Deeply interested in the expressive and psychological effects of color, Vincent chose a palette of greens and reds and yellows and violets and blues that evokes a disquieting atmosphere—one well-suited to a place of despair. He wrote to his brother, Theo, saying he used "ugly" and "deliberate" colors to express the oppressive atmosphere

Even the floor—rough, warped wood—feels hostile. The rough wooden floor would splinter if you were to walk across it barefoot. Everything in the room resists comfort. This is a place where one might lose themselves, slowly, without noise (September 1888).

The harsh overhead lights, a sickly yellow, intensify the disturbing ambiance, and the tilted floor make the scene feel unstable. The waiter all in white stands apart. Distant and unengaged, he heightens his customers sense of alienation.

The green billiard table dominating the center of the scene holds no interest for the few solitary figures slumped around the room. This café is a place where lonely people come only to linger. As shown by the late hour on the clock on the wall (12:10), these weary souls are in no hurry to leave. Van Gogh has infused this "low public house" with intense and complex emotion.

While *Terrace at Night* radiates warmth and tranquility, *Night Cafe* explores psychological despair, both show Van Gogh's ability to evoke powerful emotions through his use of color.

A refuge . . . like a sunflower standing under the sun

In the fall of 1888, Van Gogh rented a small house on the Place Lamartine in Arles which he painted yellow. The color yellow held deep emotional and symbolic significance for him and is one of the most important and recurring colors in his work. Here he envisioned warmth, sunlight, and spiritual energy, a shared studio where he could live and work alongside other artists. In this brief period before his mental breakdown, his painting of *The Yellow House* (1888) expresses optimism and hope.

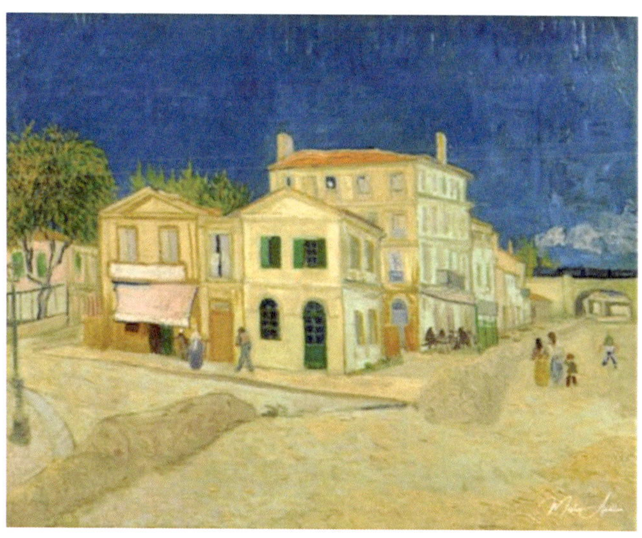

"Now that I have a house of my own, I am contented and more than contented. I can see in my mind's eye a studio and a dwelling where one can live and think and breathe a little. It is not a little. It is not a palace, but still, it is a house where my mind can find some rest, where I can invite friends, where we can work together. . .The house is painted yellow outside, with green shutters; it stands in full sunlight on the square, and with its blue sky above, it makes for a striking contrast. I want this house to become a refuge, a place where artists can share their ideas and support one another. . .I have already started making paintings of it. The brightness, the cheerfulness of the colors—I want them to show what I feel. A house that is warm, that is welcoming, that is like a sunflower standing under the sun"(September 1888).

The intense yellows and oranges contrasting with the deep blues and greens capture a welcoming sanctuary to fulfill his dream of a creative haven for himself and his artist friends.

In the foreground, the diagonal dirt mound seems to be directing the friends he hoped would come right up to his front door. The dynamic forward thrust of the road along the side of the house and the passing train in the background reinforces the sense of an open, inviting space. The town bustles with life, a world in motion—echoing Van Gogh's quiet longing as he awaits Gauguin's arrival.

Gauguin will probably come, but isn't certain yet. I have just rented, for myself alone, a four-room house, and I shall always have a room available for someone else (October 1888).

But despite this hopeful vision, the dark blue sky, the vast unknown, reflects the uncertainty of having a haven for him and his artist friends. Even the dark windows surrounded by green shutters blocking out the welcoming light on the yellow house standing "in full sunlight on the square," create a sense of emptiness and isolation, feelings that were always deep inside him and that foreshadow the end of his dream.

Hoping to build a shared artistic community at his yellow house in Arles, Van Gogh painted *In the Bedroom* (1888) as he eagerly awaited Gauguin's arrival.

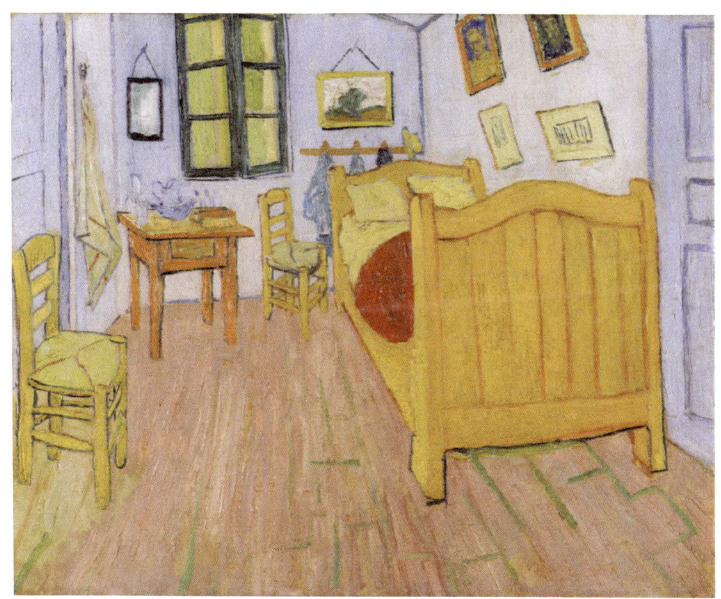

"I have done, still for my decoration, a bedroom in perspective with the furniture in broad lines, in which there is nothing but a simple wooden bed and chairs... The walls are pale violet, the floor is of red tiles, the wood of the bed and chairs is the yellow of fresh butter, the sheet and the pillows light lemon green, the coverlet blood red, the window green, the washstand orange, the basin blue, the doors lilac. I wanted to express absolute rest with these different tones" October 1888).

Experiencing a brief period of optimism, Vincent's used strong contrasting colors in his modest bedroom to evoke a sense of peace and restfulness.

"The colour must be suggestive here of rest or of sleep in general. In other words, looking at the picture should rest the brain, or rather the imagination" (October 1888).

Visually striking, the use of flat planes of color, strong outlines, and an absence of shading, clearly reflect the influence of Japanese art. The few simple pieces of furniture arranged slightly off-center, an asymmetrical element he admired in Hiroshige, creates a more dynamic space. Van Gogh often altered perspective to heighten the emotional impact.

The painting of the bedroom, again, I had certainly in mind to make it look like a Japanese print, and that by its simplicity of the arrangement (October 1888).

The furniture appears slightly off kilter, almost floating, creating a dreamlike effect. But despite his desire to create an environment of peace, rest, and harmony—"looking at the picture should rest the brain, or rather the imagination"—the tilted and slightly distorted room foreshadows his unsettling breakdown that followed so quickly. His relationship with Gauguin deteriorated, leading to his infamous ear-cutting episode in December 1888, and his dream of an artistic community unfortunately never came to fruition.

In 1884 Van Gogh mentions his painting of *The Old Church Tower at Nuenen* (1884) where his father preached traditional religious dogma he no longer felt connected to.

I've painted the old tower that rises above the fields—it's a ruin— and I wanted to express something of the idea that the church, as it stands there in the meadow, is like an empty and unenlightened preaching—the empty dark interior of the building makes it stand as a kind of dead symbol (October 1884).

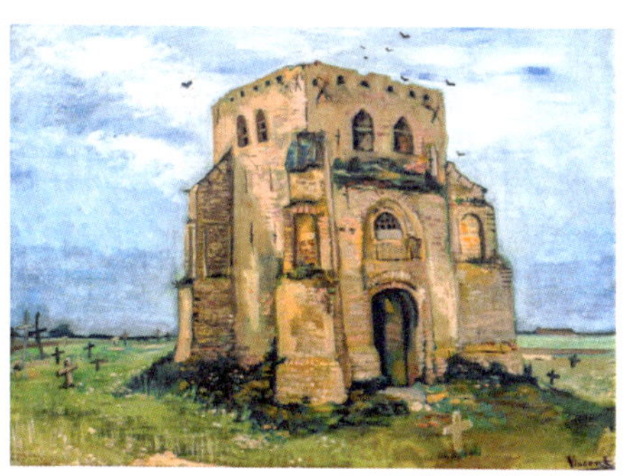

The Church at Auvers (1890) painted six years later shortly before Van Gogh's death still carries the same sentiment. At the time, he was under the care of Dr. Paul Gachet and continued to deal with deep psychological problems.

I have a larger picture of the village church—an effect in which the building appears to be violet-hued against a sky of simple deep blue colour, pure cobalt; the stained-glass windows appear as ultramarine blotches, the roof is violet and partly orange. In the foreground some green plants in bloom, and sand with the pink flow of sunshine in it. And once again it is nearly the same thing as the studies I did in Nuenen of the <u>old tower</u> and the cemetery, only it is probably that now the colour is more expressive, more sumptuous (June 1890).

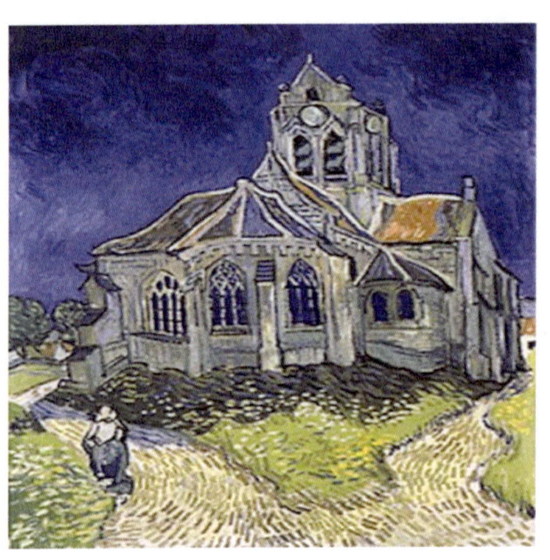

Although clearly illuminated, the church is not bathed in sunlight. Standing in its own shadow, it seems to be repelling the light—dark, looming, and isolated—rising unnaturally up to "the sky of simple deep blue colour, pure cobalt."

The dark stained-glass windows, "ultramarine blotches," reveal "the dark emptiness inside a church symbolizing "empty and unenlightened preaching." This somber presence contrasts with the bright "green plants in bloom and sand with the pink flow of sunshine in it."—a breath of fresh air, full of life and light. The distorted structure of the "violet-hued" building and the strange angles and twisting paths—everything feels off-kilter—create an eerily unstable appearance. The contrasts in the brilliant color palette combined with the signature swirling and thick brush-strokes of his late period enhances the emotional intensity. Van Gogh has created a hauntingly beautiful and expressive painting, one that strongly reveals his inner spiritual turmoil.

Caught up in his deeply personal struggles at this time, *Wheatfield with Crows* (1890), often regarded as one of Van Gogh's most iconic emotionally charged works, is considered his last completed painting.

Once back here I set to work again—though the brush almost slipped from my fingers... I painted three large canvases... They are vast fields of wheat under troubled skies, and I did need to go out of my way to express sadness and extreme loneliness... I almost think that these canvases will tell you what I cannot say in words, the health and restorative forces that I see in the country (July 1890).

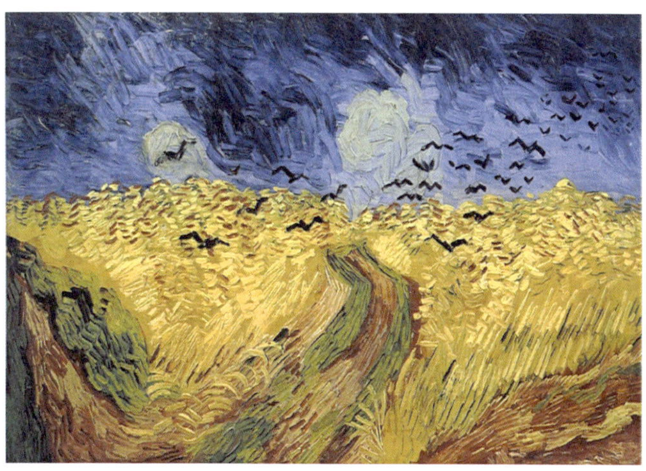

Van Gogh was deeply connected to the land and to nature. Wheatfields had personal meaning for him often associated with renewal and divinity and the eternal. The sky expressed the "infinite." However, at this critical period in his life he was battling deep depression and despair. With his future so uncertain, he wanted this painting "to express sadness and extreme loneliness." Reinforced by bold turbulent brushstrokes, the deep warm yellows and gold of the field contrasting with the cold, dark, ominous blues of the tumultuous sky, the menacing black crows and the swirling clouds create the "sadness" and "extreme loneliness" he was seeking to express.

As he stood so close to death—Vincent died six weeks later— the path, disappearing into the grain right before the horizon and the "infinite" sky, seems to be leading nowhere, suggesting the spiritual conflict he was experiencing. But the swirling white cloud just above the road which has come to an end may be affirming an "entrance into another light, one that is eternal."

In a letter to his brother in 1882 Van Gogh discussed *Tree Roots in a Sandy Ground* (1882), an earlier drawing in pencil, black chalk, ink, brown and grey wash, and opaque watercolor.

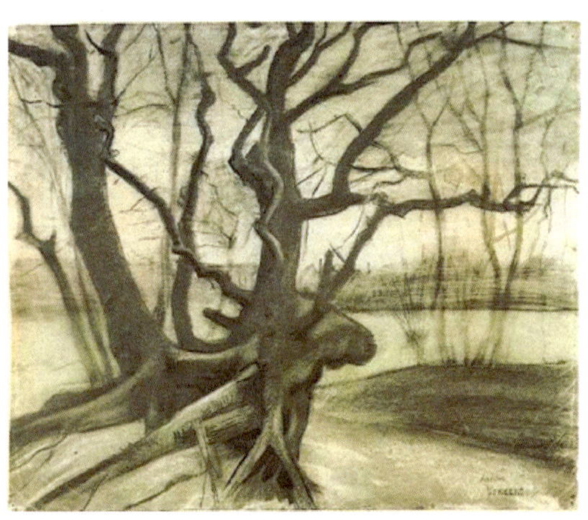

'Roots' is some tree roots in sandy ground. I've tried to imbue the landscape with the same sentiment as the figure. Frantically and fervently rooting itself, as it were, in the earth, and yet being half torn up by the storm. I wanted to express something of life's struggle (May, 1882).

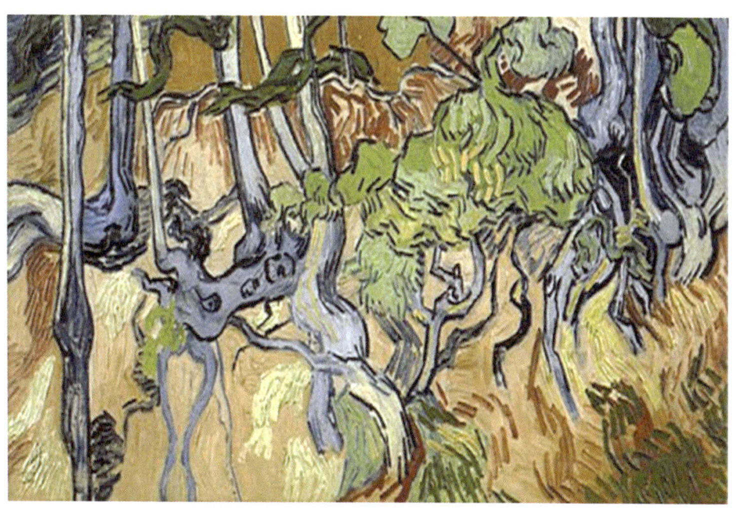

In 1890 he revisited this theme in *Tree Roots*, a significant painting often considered Van Gogh's last work before he died. The tangled, almost abstract composition reflects his psychological turmoil and the intense inner struggles he faced in his final days

The entire frame is dominated by a dense, almost abstract tangle of roots, soil, and organic forms rendered in bright colors. The thick brush strokes—a chaotic swirl of greens and blues and ochers—heighten the emotional intensity. The cropped, close-up composition emphasizes the intricate, underlying patterns and abstraction. Visually and conceptually ahead of its time, the painting borders on modern abstract art.

Vincent Van Gogh died a few days later on July 29, 1890 at age 37. His last words to his brother were:

"*La tristesse durera toujours*"
"*The sadness will last forever.*"

Though these words express the deep sorrow he carried to the end of his life, his soul lives on in the joy of the magnificent legacy he left to us.

How much there is in art that is beautiful. If only one can remember what one has seen, one is never empty or truly lonely, and never alone.—(July,1883

His footprints—resilient and growing stronger with each passing day—continue to resonate. They inspire artists across movements and generations to explore color, emotional depth, transformation, and the "pure harmony and music" they hear—the personal truth of who they are—through their own work.

Source of Illustrations

Self-Portrait Van Gogh, Vincent 1889. Wikimedia Commons.

Still Life with Bible Van Gogh, Vincent 1885. Wikimedia Commons.

The Potato Eaters Van Gogh, Vincent 1885. Wikimedia Commons.

The Sower Millet, Jean Francois 1850. Museum of Fine Arts, Boston. Wikimedia Commons.

The Sower at Sunset Van Gogh, Vincent. 1888. Wikimedia Commons.

The Sower (with a cut tree Trunk Van Gogh, Vincent,.1888. Wikimedia Commons.

Noon: Rest from Work Millet, Jean François 1866. Museum of Fine Arts, Boston. Wikimedia Commons.

The Siesta Van Gogh, Vincent. 1890. *Wikimedia Commons,*

Starry Night Van Gogh, Vincent 1889. courtesy of Google Art Project. via Wikimedia Commons.

The Great Wave off Kanagawa. Hokusai 1831 as part of his series *Thirty-Six Views of Mount Fuji.* The Metropolitan Museum of Art.

Starry Night over the Rhone Van Gogh, Vincent. 1888. Wikimedia Commons.

Road with Cypresses Van Gogh, Vincent. 1890.The Metropolitan Museum of Art, New York. Photograph by author, 2023.

La Berceuse Van Gogh, Vincent 1890. Metropolitan Museum of Art.

Sunflowers Van Gogh, Vincent 1888. Wikimedia Commons.

A Portrait of a Bridge (after Hiroshige) Van Gogh, Vincent 1887. Metropolitan Museum of Art.

A Bridge in the Rain -Hiroshige 1857. Metropolitan Museum of Art.

Plum Garden at Kameido – Hiroshige 1830-1833. (From Thirty-six Views of Mt. Fuji. Wikimedia Commons.

Flowering Plum Orchard (after Hiroshige) Van Gogh, Vincent 1887. Wikimedia Commons.

Fields with Irises Van Gogh, Vincent 1888.Wikimedia Commons.

Irises at Horikiri – Hiroshige 1857 from One Hundred Views of Edo. The Metropolitan Museum of Art.

Fishing Boats on the Beach at Saintes-Maries Van Gogh, Vincent 1888. Wikimedia Commons.

Fishing Boats at Fukagawa -Hokusai *in Kai Province* (from *Thirty-six Views of Mount Fuji*). The Metropolitan Museum. Wikimedia Commons.

Almond Blossom Van Gogh, Vincent 1890. Wikimedia Commons.

Irises Van Gogh, Vincent 1889. Wikimedia Commons.

Irises and Butterfly – Hiroshige. Edo Period 1830-1844. Wikimedia Commons.

Langlois Bridge at Arles with Women. Van Gogh, Vincent 1888. Wikimedia Commons.

The Drum Bridge at Meguro and Sunset- Hokusai 1830-1832. The Metropolitan Museum. Wikimedia Commons.

Pollard Willow. Van Gogh, Vincent. 1882. Wikimedia Commons.

A View of Arles. Van Gogh, Vincent 1888. Wikimedia Commons.

The Courtyard of the Hospital at Arles Van Gogh, Vincent 1889. Wikimedia Commons.

Olive Trees with Cut Trunk Van Gogh, Vincent Minneapolis Institute of Art. via Wikimedia Commons

The Pine Grove of Miho in Suruga Province -Hiroshige from Famous Views of the Sixty-odd Provinces. Wikimedia Commons.

Olive Trees with Yellow Sky and Sun Van Gogh, Vincent 1889. Wikimedia Commons.

Women Picking Olives Van Gogh, Vincent 1889. The Metropolitan Museum. Of Art. Wikimedia Commons.

A Pork-Butcher's Shop Seen From a Window Van Gogh, Vincent 1888. Wikimedia Commons.

At Eternity's Gate Van Gogh, Vincent 1890. Wikimedia Commons.

Self-Portrait as a Bonze Dedicated to Gauguin Van Gogh, Vincent 1888. Wikimedia Commons.

Portrait of Hokusai - Keisai Eisen. Wikimedia commons.

Self-Portrait with a Bandaged Ear Van Gogh, Vincent 1889. Wikimedia Commons.

The Peasant (Patience Escalier Van Gogh, Vincent 1888. Wikimedia Commons.

The Poet (Portrait of Eugene Boch) Van Gogh, Vincent 1888. Wikimedia Commons.

Portrait of Dr. Gachet Van Gogh, Vincent 1890, Wikimedia Commons.

The Night Café Van Gogh, Vincent 1888. Wikimedia Commons.

Terrace at Night Van Gogh, Vincent 1888. Wikimedia Commons.

The Yellow House Van Gogh, Vincent 1888. Wikimedia Commons.

In the Bedroom Van Gogh, Vincent 1888. Wikimedia Commons.

The Old Church Tower and Cemetery Van Gogh, Vincent 1884. Wikimedia Commons.

The Church at Auvers Van Gogh, Vincent 1890. Wikimedia Commons.

Wheatfield with Crows Van Gogh, Vincent 1890. Wikimedia Commons.

Tree Roots in Sandy Ground Van Gogh, Vincent 1882. Wikimedia Commons.

Tree Roots Van Gogh, Vincent 1890. Wikimedia Commons.

Works Cited

Aurier, G. Albert. "The Isolated Ones." Published in *Mercure de France*. January, 1890

Bashō, Matsuo. *On Love and Barley: Haiku of Basho*. Translated by Lucien Stryk, Penguin Books, 1985.

Carlyle, Thomas. *On Heroes, Hero-Worship, and the Heroic in History*. Edited by Carl Niemeyer, University of Nebraska Press, 1966.

Crane, Hart. *Complete Poems and Selected Letters.* Edited by Langdon Hammer, Library of America, 2006.

Elderfield, John. *The "Wild Beasts": Fauvism and Its Affinities*. New York: Museum of Modern Art, 1976.

Easwaran, E. (Trans.). (2007). *The Upanishads*. Nilgiri Press.

Shapiro, Meyer. *Modern Art: 19th and 20th Centuries*. George Barzillen, 1998

The Holy Bible: King James Version. (2024). King James Bible Online.

Van Gogh, Vincent. *The Letters of Vincent van Gogh*. Edited by Mark Roskill, Penguin Classics, 2003. Also available online.

Whitman, Walt. *Leaves of Grass*. Edited by Michael Moon. Modern Library. 2000

Zola, Émile. *The Experimental Novel, and Other Essays*. Translated by Belle M. Sherman, Cassell and Company, 1893

Anne Dupré

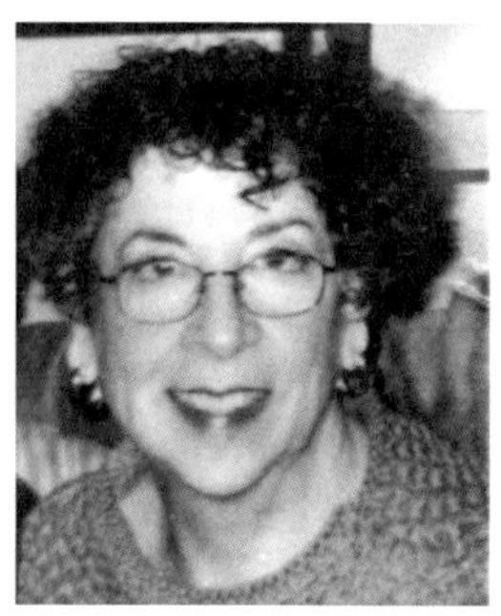

I don't know exactly when my love for Van Gogh's paintings first began, but it has increased over the years. Recently I went to the special Van Gogh exhibit at the National Gallery of Art in London—a truly wonderful experience. A few days after I returned home to New York, I sat down at my computer and began to write. The journey has been so illuminating and so elevating that I am anxious to share it with others who also love Van Gogh's art, and I am sure there are very few who don't. Using his references to his paintings in the deeply absorbing letters he wrote to his brother Theo, letters that unfold the inner workings of his creative life and reveal his intention and his state of mind, has given me an in-depth understanding of both the artist and his brilliant work.

Retired English Professor at Molloy University

Publications:

The Little Pug's Dream
It's Time to Tell a Story
The Brightest Star in the Sky
Where Dreams Live

9 781945 432712